DEDICATION

This book is dedicated to my wife, Lynnie, who has shared this incredible trip, just two love-struck vagabonds wandering the back roads of life.

TABLE OF CONTENTS

Acknowledgments

Credits

Introduction

About Ghosts and Hauntings

SECTION ONE
IN THE STEEL CITY

1. Point State Park..1

2. Point Park University...7

3. Macy's Department Store....................................9

4. William Penn Hotel..12

5. Bridge of Sighs and Old Allegheny County Jail....15

6. Duquesne University..19

7. Mercy Hospital...23

8. The Pittsburgh Playhouse..................................26

9. The University of Pittsburgh..................................31

10. Carnegie Library and Museum............................35

11. Chatham University. 38

11. Clayton, the Home of Henry Clay Frick................42

SECTION TWO
IN THE SUBURBS, EXURBS, AND
COUNTRYSIDE

12. The George Westinghouse Bridge........................47

13. Old Brush Creek Cemetery...................................50

14. Seton Hill University...53

15. Westmoreland County Courthouse Square...........56

16. St. Xavier Convent and School.............................59

17. St. Vincent College..62

18. Lincoln Highway Heritage Corridor......................67

19. Lady of the Lake...71

20. The Ligonier Tavern...73

21. The Broken Oak..77

22. Fort Ligonier's Lost Soldier....................................80

23. Ghost on Laurel Mountain....................................82

24. Dead Man's Curve..83

25. North Star High School..86

26. Flight 93 National Memorial................................88

27. The S.S. Grandview...94

28. Bedford's Best Bordello.......................................97

29. The Jean Bonnet Inn..104

30. Quaker Schoolhouse at Old Bedford Village.......109

31. The Face in the Window....................................112

SECTION THREE
THE CENTER OF THE STATE

32. Pond Bank, south of Fayetteville......................115

33. The Cashtown Inn..117

34. Herr Tavern and Publick House..............................122

35. Gettysburg...127

36. The High Water Mark at Gettysburg....................130

37. York College..134

38. The Old Abandoned Prison at York.......................136

39. The Phantom Biker of York....................................138

40. Camp Security...141

41. Eastern York High School......................................143

42. The Accomac Inn..146

SECTION FOUR
APPROACHING THE CITY OF
BROTHERLY LOVE

43. Lancaster County Prison..148

44. Franklin and Marshall College..............................150

45. The Fulton Opera House..152

46. Main Street, Strasburg..159

47. The Ship Inn..161

48. The Radnor Hotel.......... 163

49. Cabrini College...165

SECTION FIVE
IN THE CITY OF BROTHERLY LOVE

50. Villanova University.................................169

51. Bryn Mawr College..................................172

52. Rosemont College....................................174

53. General Wayne Inn..................................176

54. Eastern State Penitentiary.......................180

55. Bonaparte's Court..................................182

56 St. Peter's Episcopal Church Cemetery...............184

57. Washington Square..................................186

58. City Tavern...189

Visiting the Ghosts of Route 30.....................................192

About The Author..197

ACKNOWLEDGMENTS

A book like this is never the work of only one person. I have received invaluable editorial assistance and encouragement from the members of the Greensburg Writers Group. It is indeed a privilege to be counted in the membership of such a talented group of writers, who are responsible for well over one hundred published books.

    I would like to thank everyone who graciously shared their ghostly experiences. Thanks to Jan McLaughlin for sharing both her encounter and her picture of the otherworldly patron at the bar in the Ligonier Tavern and to Keven P. for his experience at the High Water Mark at Gettysburg. Thanks to Carolyn Rogers for use of the Ice House Photo. To Diana Hunt, thank you for allowing me to use your story about the ghost of Laurel Mountain. Special thanks to Patty Wilson for allowing me to use portions of her story "Jean Bonnet Tavern Revisited," from her excellent collection *The Pennsylvania Ghost Guide, Vol. 1*. Mary Ann Mogus, thank you for sharing your paranormal experience at St. Xavier's with us. Bev LaGorga, thank you so much for allowing the use of the excerpt from your book, *"The Making of a Psychic – We Don't Talk About Those Kind Of Things."*

    And, Paisley Adams, thank you so much for allowing me the use of your wonderful poem, "Gettysburg."

My undying gratitude goes out to Judith Gallagher of Gallagher Editorial Services, whose editorial pencil has made this book readable. Any typos that have crept in to this book have arrived unnanounced as a result of my own inadequacies and in no way reflect on her editing skills.

The cover art is by Linda Ciletti, yet one more example of her wonderful graphic artistry. Drop by her website at www.lindaciletti.net for a visit.

CREDITS

All of the illustrations and photographs in this book are the original work of the author, except as noted:

Page #1 Modified photo of fountain at Point State Park, Pittsburgh, PA. Used under Creative Commons Licensure. See www.creativecommons.org/licenses/by/2.0/deed.en.

Page #48 Modified photo of Ice House at Lady of the Lake B & B. Taken by Carolyn Rogers. Used with permission

Page # 51 Photo of apparition in barroom of the Ligonier Tavern. Taken by Jan McLaughlin. Used with permission.

Page #63 Modified photo of SS Grandview. Taken by National Park Service employee. Public domain.

INTRODUCTION: US ROUTE 30

US Route 30 shares a large portion of its roadway with the Lincoln Highway and runs from Atlantic City, New Jersey, to Astoria, Oregon. It was the country's first coast-to-coast road.

Route 30 through Pennsylvania is haunted. Of that, there is no doubt. I concern myself with those hauntings that occur along its original route from the Point in Pittsburgh to Independence Hall in Philadelphia.

On March 18 of 1816, Pittsburgh was incorporated as a city. Twenty-three months later, February 18, 1818, saw the opening of the Pittsburgh-Harrisburg Turnpike. This was the forerunner of Route 30. Of course, by that time, the road was already haunted by various and sundry deceased individuals, including Indians, settlers, and soldiers. They were later joined by farmers, students, workers, suicides, and lovers, all no longer partaking of this mortal coil but unable or unwilling to leave it.

Historic Route 30 meanders along one-way city streets, making turns at various intersections for no apparent reason. It goes out of its way to bisect every little hamlet, borough, and township along the way from Pittsburgh to Philadelphia. Sometimes it runs over mountains, sometimes around them. It depends on the whim of the original teamsters who traveled it. They depended on the savvy of those who originally trod that path, the Indian tribes of Pennsylvania. They left track marks in the mud and everyone else, thinking that was the best way to go, followed along. Then someone else came along, saw the rough road, and paved it. This is the route we will follow.

The route has many names. In the Pittsburgh area it is called Penn Avenue, Forbes Avenue, Main Street, Pittsburgh Street, Ardmore Boulevard and a few others. As it travels across the state, Lincoln Highway, Penn-Lincoln Highway, and Forbes Trail are the names it shares. The Philadelphia end of the state mostly calls it Lancaster Pike and Lancaster Avenue. Of course, given its penchant for running right through the middle of little and medium-sized towns, Main Street is one of its favorite names.

The Route 30 in this book is not the Route 30 that you will find on the official Pennsylvania Highway Map. The route on that map includes parkways, bypasses, circular routes around towns, limited-access freeways, and four-lane monstrosities that cater to the traveling public's desire to avoid the absorption of local atmosphere at any cost. God forbid that they actually come into contact with something other than concrete, lane markers, and those hardy trees that give the illusion of forest.

We will travel historic Route 30 through six Pennsylvania counties designated the Lincoln Highway Heritage Corridor. This section of the highway has become a 200-mile long museum celebrating the country's first transcontinental road.

I heartily recommend that anyone traveling this section purchase *The Lincoln Highway, Pennsylvania Traveler's Guide* by Brian Bunko. This book and other historical highway publications are available through the Lincoln Highway Heritage Commission's website at www.lhhc.org.

While traveling this great road, follow the advice of the Lincoln Highway Heritage Commission and "Keep Thinkin' Lincoln!"

Let's get going.

ABOUT GHOSTS AND HAUNTINGS

Webster says that a ghost is "the specter of a person appearing after death, an apparition." A whole bunch of entries later, Webster says that to be haunted is "to be frequented by ghosts, spirits, etc." If it's good enough for Webster, it's good enough for me. That "etc.," gives me pause, however.

The great majority of the hauntings along Route 30 are of the ghostly persuasion. They range from the shades of infants to those of historical figures and everything in between. And the great preponderance of them died in a way that most coroners would not call "natural causes."

Webster just tells us what, not why. For some reason or other, these people have unfinished business in this plane of existence. They must accomplish something before they can go on. Maybe there is a message that must be delivered, or a murderer caught, or a warning issued. Some look for their lost children. Many just weren't ready to die. It was a shock to their systems in more ways than one. One thing we can be sure of is that intense emotions were involved.

The most haunted locations tell us that. Where are emotions more intense than in prisons and hospitals, where life and death meet each other on a daily basis? How about institutions of higher learning, where a person's whole future can hinge on one passing grade? Then there is the compounded shame of an unwed mother who takes not only her life, but that of her unborn child as well. How about the emotions generated when 100,000 young men clash with the sole purpose of eliminating one another? Robbery and murder, unrequited love, and jealousy are all part of the hauntings. Are we starting to see a pattern?

What about that "etc?" Those shadow beasts come under that heading. So do ghostly trains, trucks, and landlocked ocean liners. What are they? A projection from the past or something that originated in the brain of the observer? Could be, but that wouldn't account for the similarity of the observations. If there's one thing I've learned researching this book, it's that locations where emotions run strong produce haunts.

The only way I can learn about ghosts and their locations is for people to tell me. Future endeavors will include subsequent editions of "Route 30: Pennsylvania's Haunted Highway," as well as books about the hauntings along Route 22, Route 6, and the coal country of PA. While I cannot afford to pay for stories, anyone who furnishes me with one that gets into print will receive credit in the book for the story. And an autographed copy of the book.

You can reach me at ed@ekelemen.com and visit with me at my website: www.ekelemen.com.

Read on and enjoy.

Ed Kelemen

I

In The Steel City

Point State Park

Pittsburgh

Pittsburgh's huge fountain is the focal point of the convergence of the Monongahela and Allegheny rivers to create the mighty Ohio, the nation's first superhighway.

As recently as 300 years ago, the only feet that trod the forested juncture of rivers were encased in moccasins.

These belonged to the people who husbanded and kept the area pristine for over 13,000 years. The first were members of the Mound Builders. Then came the Hopewell culture. Then the Iroquois, Lenape, and Shawnee, all tribes who had been displaced by European settlers to the east and south. They had been devastated by those diseases that the Europeans brought with them. It's no wonder that many of their spirits chose to remain behind rather than infect the afterworld with the white man's diseases.

Pittsburgh's first incarnation was a short-lived one as Fort St. George under British rule. After that Major George Washington politely asked the French military presence to leave the area. A few months later, in April 1754, when the fort was barely half built, 500 Frenchmen returned. They evicted the British settlers who had come from Virginia. Then they built Fort Duquesne on the same spot. They were able to hold it for only four years. In 1758, General John Forbes retook it from the French, built a new fort there, and christened it Fort Pitt. This didn't happen without the loss of many Indian, French, and British lives. Their spirits imbued what would come to be known as the Point District.

This small British foothold at the headwaters of the Ohio River grew and grew. The town that sprung up around the fort was named Pittsburgh. Since it was the jumping-off place for the myriad of pioneers heading into the sunset to settle America, it was called "The Gateway to the West." A large industry grew here, manufacturing keelboats for those settlers. They traveled the Ohio in those keelboats. When they decided to strike westward overland, the keelboats were dismantled, then reassembled into wagons. On July 15, 1802 Meriwether

Lewis and William Clark departed Pittsburgh on their journey of exploration to find a transcontinental water route to the Northwest Territories. By that time, the Point District was a jumble of small manufacturing plants and wharves devoted to the keelboat industry.

Some enterprising souls discovered that the Pittsburgh area was ideally suited for the manufacture of iron. The surrounding mountains were full of ore, and the forests of Western Pennsylvania provided the necessary fuel to stoke the furnaces. An inexhaustible supply of coal was discovered in the Appalachian Range, and the rivers were the highways to deliver all these supplies. Pittsburgh was reborn as the Iron City. Its population went from around 1,500 in 1800 to 50,000 in 1860. During his 1842 visit to the city, Charles Dickens described it as "Hell with the lid off." The Point District devolved into a mishmash of warehouses, foundries, brothels, saloons, and derelict hotels. It existed to serve the iron-smelting industry.

Pittsburgh garnered a new nickname, the Smoky City. Two things brought boom times to Pittsburgh: the railroad and the American Civil War. By the war's end, the city of Pittsburgh was producing over half of the United States' steel. A third of the country's glass production took place here as well.

Pittsburgh was reborn again, this time as the Steel City, but the derogatory appellation Smoky City stayed on. Now the Point District, in addition to everything else, was crisscrossed with railroad tracks. Things went for another hundred years, with pollution becoming worse and worse.

By the twentieth century, office workers who wore white shirts had to bring at least two shirts a day to work.

By noon, the first shirt would be too coated with soot to present a professional appearance. Lower-echelon clerks brought extra white collars made of stiffened cardboard and carried chunks of chalk to periodically whiten those collars during the artificial overcast that passed for daylight. Streetlights were required, even by day.

By the middle of the twentieth century, the air was so thick that it could be cut with a knife and its overlay of sulfur dioxide gave it the essence of rotten eggs. Finally, in the 1950s, a governor and past mayor of Pittsburgh, David L. Lawrence, amassed enough political power to do what had to be done. He made it his life's work to eradicate, once and for all, the city's reputation as the Smoky City.

The Point was a dingy eyesore of slums, warehouses, and derelict buildings, but Lawrence envisioned a Golden Triangle, a showplace of modern skyscrapers, office buildings, and hotels in a park-like setting. He had quite a bit of opposition in this endeavor. A huge portion of the distressed area was owned by influential people in the city's hierarchy. But Lawrence, along with his banking mogul ally, Richard K. Mellon, steamrolled that opposition. Property after property was acquired by eminent domain and bulldozed to clear the way for the Golden Triangle.

Finally, all that was left to acquire was a small knot of warehouses right in the middle of the area to be rebuilt. The owners were adamant; they wouldn't move. Fortuitously, a fire of unknown origin destroyed those buildings one night, and the last impediment to the construction of the Golden Triangle was removed.

The original outlines of the Fort Pitt Blockhouse and bastions were rediscovered. Two new double-deck multilane bridges were built linking Pittsburgh with places north and south on newly created interstate highways, and a brand new park dubbed Point State Park was built on the site. Its huge fountain announced Pittsburgh's Renaissance to the world, washing away the old identity of soot, grime, and smoke. Serenity lay where chaos used to reign.

Along with that serenity came some of the area's earliest settlers. As a concession to modern times, the whole area around the Blockhouse and Fort is ringed with security cameras. Security officers are reluctant to talk about some of the things they see on those monitors during the late night hours. People dressed in nineteenth-century and early twentieth-century garb, looking as though they are headed to or from work. Men swinging that emblem of the industrial laborer, the lunch pail. Women dressed as maids, washerwomen, or cleaners. Forays to evict these people from the museum grounds always meet with failure because the trespassers are never seen in the flesh.

A beautiful park in the center of a bustling city attracts other trespassers as well. These are the homeless ones of the city. When the weather is agreeable, their numbers increase on the paths, byways, and undersides of bridge ramps within the park, where they congregate and exchange stories of the apparitions they encounter. Those apparitions include frontiersmen, George Washington himself, Indians, and indistinct specters in the mists of the riverbanks. The police officers who are sent to deal with these squatters aren't too fast to discount their stories. Some of them have been treated to encounters with those same spirits of times long gone.

If you find yourself strolling along in the twilight of evening or in the mist of a newly dawned day in the direction of the fountain approaching the bridge overpass, keep your wits about you. That frontiersman leaning against a tree or that 19th century lady hurrying off to work is neither imaginary nor a re-enactor. You may even encounter the father of our country as he prepares his troops for the retreat to Fort Necessity.

***

Let's drive along the path that Route 30 traveled before the days of superhighways. Heading east on Commonwealth Place, we'll cross Liberty Avenue, and then hang a left onto the Boulevard of the Allies. When the Parkway East opened on October 15, 1953, Route 30 was redirected onto the Boulevard and then onto the Parkway, saving 30 to 45 minutes of rambling around on streetcar-congested city streets.

But we're going the old way, so we'll hang another left onto Smithfield Street, once the center of the city's downtown retail commercial district.

Three blocks on Smithfield Street and we are at the site of the old Kaufmannn's Department Store, operating under the Macy's banner since 2005.

Ed Kelemen

Point Park University

201 Wood Street
Pittsburgh

Lawrence Hall, located at the corner of Wood Street and the Boulevard of the Allies has had a few incarnations. It was originally the home of the Keystone Athletic Club, evolving into the Keystone Hotel. In 1955, the Sheraton Corporation took it over and renamed it the Sheraton Pittsburgh, a showplace of a hotel. Then it became the Sherwyn Hotel, still an address of distinction.

Retired Pennsylvania State Supreme Court Justice Michael Musmanno was known for serving in two world wars, rising to the top of his chosen field as a participant in the legal process, and his life-long antipathy toward the idea that anyone other than Christopher Columbus discovered America. He was also a long-time resident of the Sherwyn Hotel, calling room 1917 home until his death on Columbus Day, 1968. He even refused to be relocated when the University, then a college, took over the building for use as office space and dormitory rooms in 1967. He happily coexisted with the students, often genially interacting with them.

When he passed on in October of 1968, his earthly remains were interred at Arlington National Cemetery as befitted a Rear Admiral of the United States Navy. His non-corporeal remains however decided to stay on at the building where he had enjoyed his final years, now called Lawrence Hall.

He is credited with shuffling along the halls in his afterlife as he did in life. The sounds of feet shuffling along the halls unaided by earthly influences has earned him the nickname, "the Shuffler." He also gets the blame with students are forced to wait interminably for elevators that glide by their floors without stopping. The upper floor dorm inhabitants have been treated to their doors slamming shut inexplicably.

Justice Musmanno, ever a maverick in life seems to have found a gentle way to prod the imaginations of students even to this day nearly a half-century later.

A block farther along the Boulevard of the Allies and a left onto Smithfield Street will lead us to another famous Pittsburgh landmark...

Ed Kelemen

Macy's Department Store

400 Fifth Avenue
Pittsburgh

In 1871, the Kaufmannn brothers, Isaac and Jacob, opened a relatively small men's clothing store on the South Side of Pittsburgh. Six years later, they moved to this central location in downtown Pittsburgh. Known as the Big Store, it was owned and operated for most of the 20th century by Edgar J. Kaufmann. You may have heard of one of Mr. Kaufmann's other properties, Fallingwater. It was designed by world-famous architect Frank Lloyd Wright and is located some 50 miles south of Pittsburgh.

Kaufmann's was Pittsburgh's most successful department store. It watched all of its competitors fall by the wayside and has been operating under the Macy's name since 2005. But to this day, Pittsburghers still call it Kaufmann's.

The building housing the store was built on the ground where Grant's Hill once was located. Grant's Hill was named after British Major James Grant, who was defeated by a coalition of French colonists and indigenous Indians from Fort Duquesne on September 14, 1758. As Downtown expanded, more and more of Grant's Hill was cut away to be used for building.

The tenth floor of the building was the ground level at the time of the battle. One of Major Grant's Highlanders who was killed during the battle haunts that tenth floor. Night cleaning staffers often hear his footsteps marching back and forth on the tiled floor while ghostly bag piping floats on the still air.

I have tried but have been unable to hear anything on that floor during store hours. The din of shoppers, background music, and cash registers overcomes anything ethereal.

***

Unfortunately, Forbes Avenue is one-way the wrong way right here, so we've a bit of trekking to do. Let's keep going straight on Smithfield Street. In one block, we'll come to Fifth Avenue. At this intersection is the famous Kaufmannn's Clock, the place for generations of Pittsburghers to meet. Many people over the years heard the admonition, "Meet me under Kaufmannn's Clock." As the ultimate indignity, people often invite foes to kiss them--and not on the lips-- at Pittsburgh's most public place.

We've got to go another block on Smithfield Street, then make a right turn onto Oliver Avenue. This complication would be unnecessary except for the city fathers' penchant for arbitrarily putting up "No Right Turn" signs and deeming streets one-way for no apparent reason. One block on Oliver Avenue and we turn right again, this time onto William Penn Place.

If you're energetic enough to be on foot, skip that last. Just take a right onto Fifth Avenue. One block ahead on our left is William Penn Place.

Pennsylvania's Haunted Route 30

William Penn Hotel

530 William Penn Place
Pittsburgh

To enter the William Penn Hotel is to take a trip back in time, back to the days of fabled opulence, the hotels of Bogart and Bacall movies. Just walking in the main entrance treats you to polished marble ceilings that stretch to infinity and fabulous murals depicting the city's history.

You will tread the same floors and eat in the same restaurants that witnessed history being made by presidents from Herbert Hoover to Dwight D. Eisenhower, John F. Kennedy, and Lyndon B. Johnson. Entertainment giants such as Bob Hope and Lawrence

Welk had life-changing experiences here. Welk's signature champagne bubble machine was invented by the staff. In 1934 Bob Hope proposed to his wife in this hotel

The William Penn was built in 1916 by Henry Clay Frick, one of the richest and most influential men of his time, who wanted a world-class luxury hotel in Pittsburgh. It was expanded in 1929 to become the second-largest hotel in the world.

The most expensive rooms in the hotel at the time of its opening, the seven-room State Suite, went for $50 per night. Regular rooms rented for $2.50 per night. Today these same rooms start at about $190 per night. The luxury suites rent for quite a bit more.

During the hotel's heyday, it required a huge staff, mostly of young women, to run the place seamlessly. This was in the early twentieth century, when ladies were considered to be the weaker sex. Young women had to be protected from the unwanted, uncouth, and uncivilized. So the twenty-second and twenty-third floors of this massive monument to luxury was set aside as dormitories for them.

Imagine what it must have been like to be a young woman getting your first job at the William Penn Hotel. Not only were you working at the most luxurious hotel in the country, you actually got to live there!

Despite the good intentions of the hotel's management, this attempt at protection came to naught. One of these young ladies was murdered in the dormitory. Ever since, night staffers feel cold gusts of wind chilling them and sense that they are being watched. They also hear footsteps and shrill laughter when no one else is there.

Mrs. N., a longtime supervisor of cleaning services at the hotel, told me that she has personally felt a malevolent presence in those hallways and has found cleaning supplies disturbed when no one should have been there. "Ed," she said, "I have always told my trainees to stay off the top two floors. You got no business being there, and bad things can happen." She didn't expand on exactly what she meant.

For whatever reason, to this day, those two floors are not used for guest rooms.

***

At the end of the block, turn left onto Fifth Avenue and travel two blocks before making a right turn onto Ross Street. We are now between two ancient buildings that resemble medieval castles. On the left is the old Allegheny County Jail and on the right is the Allegheny County Courthouse.

Connecting these two imposing edifices is the Bridge of Sighs.

Ed Kelemen

The Bridge of Sighs and the Old Allegheny County Jail

Ross Street
Pittsburgh

The original Allegheny County lockup on Ross Street has had a number of noteworthy incidents take place within its walls since it opened for business in 1884. Possibly the most infamous incident happened in February 1902, when Katherine Soffel, the wife of warden Peter Soffel, helped a pair of convicted murderers escape. While the two Biddle brothers, Ed and Jack,

15

awaited their execution, a romance developed between Ed Biddle and Kate Soffel. She smuggled them a gun and they escaped, shooting a guard. The brothers were killed in a shootout a few days later. Kate was wounded. She was tried for her part in the escape and spent several years within the walls of the lockup as a prisoner.

During those years, there was an actual murderers' row at the jail, where condemned prisoners and those awaiting trial for capital offenses were housed. The *New York Times* of September 15, 1907, reported the following incident under the headline, "Murderers Saw a Ghost."

A certain W. A. Culp had recently moved into murderers' row to await trial on charges that he had murdered his brother. For whatever reason (fear of the unknown or maybe remorse), he committed suicide the week before the article appeared in the paper. He was neither the first nor the last prisoner to commit suicide within the confines of that granite edifice. Most of those who did so saw it as a way out. What made W. A. Culp different was that he stayed on murderers' row. At the time of his demise, fourteen other prisoners were awaiting their fate in that prison within a prison. To a man, they complained about sharing their accommodations with the ghost of W. A. Culp. They said that he came back each night and prevented them from sleeping. They were so vociferous in their complaints that Warden Lewis moved murderers' row to another part of the prison.

**

Take a look at the stone arched footbridge leading between the old jail and the courthouse. Inmates were taken from the old county jail to the courthouse and back over that bridge. Those going to the courthouse were hoping that the legal system would set them free. Even prisoners who committed their crimes in front of an audience protested their innocence on the way to trial. Those coming back to the jail were in the throes of despair. Perhaps they couldn't arrange bail, or they were sentenced to the jail for a short stay after being found guilty of a minor offense. Some of them were going back to gather up their belongings before heading for a long stay in a state or federal penitentiary. A few of them had an appointment with the executioner.

Small wonder, then, that this walkway acquired the appellation the Bridge of Sighs, after the original one in Venice, Italy. There condemned prisoners were given a choice while they traversed the bridge on the way to their execution. They could either enter the prison, where the execution order would be carried out, or throw themselves off the bridge into the river while wearing chains and manacles. While a number of prisoners avoided execution in this manner, I have heard of none who survived the jump.

While the jail was in use, nobody ever experienced anything on the bridge other than the extreme emotions of the prisoners. Since the jail was moved to a modern, more humane facility, the old jail has been used for the juvenile and family sections of Common Pleas Court.
The raucous sounds of 500-plus inmates squabbling, playing music, and just generally moving about aren't there any more to drown out sounds leaking from the other side. Since 1995, when the new jail opened a few blocks away, the night cleaning staffers at the courthouse hear hushed conversations, shuffling footsteps, and

muted cries of anguish. This occurs only in the area of the Bridge of Sighs, nowhere else. It's as though the very masonry of the bridge has been infused with 109 years' worth of extreme emotions that are only now making themselves known.

***

Take the next left turn and we'll be on Forbes Avenue. After zigging, zagging, jigging, and jogging all over downtown Pittsburgh, we are finally back on Forbes Avenue, Route 30's original path. In a few blocks we'll pass the Armstrong Tunnels on our right. Immediately after them, McAnulty Drive will be on our right, leading us onto Duquesne University's campus.

Ed Kelemen

Duquesne University

600 Forbes Avenue
Pittsburgh

Duquesne University was founded on October 1, 1878, as the Pittsburgh Catholic College by the Rev. Joseph Straub and the congregation of the Holy Ghost. Classes for that first group of 40 students and 6 instructors were held above a bakery on Wylie Avenue in the Hill District. Duquesne expanded to its current campus on the Bluff and built the Old Main building in 1885. This five-story red-brick landmark was for years the highest point on the Pittsburgh skyline. It is still used as the administrative building on campus.

Over the years, this fine old institution of learning has become home to a number of haunts. Maybe the name of the group that founded it has attracted some of them.

Old Main is haunted by specters and echoes of the Underground Railroad. Its basement was a major station of that route to freedom. By the time slaves reached this point of their journey, they were well on the way to freedom. Even so, some were captured there and returned to slavery. Doors in the basement open and close with no corporeal assistance, and lights turn themselves on and off there. Murmuring voices are heard through the building's air vents, and rattling chains resound along the halls.

However, Old Main was completed in 1885, long after the Underground Railroad ceased to exist. Two possible explanations are set forward to explain this anomaly. The first is that Old Main is built over the remains of a previous structure on Boyd's Hill, the Bluff's former name. The second is that, since Old Main was for years the highest point on the Pittsburgh skyline, it attracted the anguished spirits of those slaves who never made it to freedom on their northward journey over Boyd's Hill.

Saint Ann Hall was built in 1964 as a freshman residence, with males in one wing and females in the opposite wing. University policy requires that freshmen and sophomores reside on-campus or at home with their parents. This is supposed to provide a distraction-free atmosphere conducive to learning.

Imagine a freshman girl who has just escaped family life and the aggravations of younger siblings. Here she is out on her own for the first time. She gets assigned to room #409. She is minding her own business, perhaps studying for a quiz, eating a snack and sipping a soda, enjoying the solitude. Suddenly a young boy appears in the room, throws things all over the place, then disappears before she can even admonish him. This mischievous ghost has been haunting this particular room for years.

The former headquarters of Fisher Scientific sits across Forbes Avenue from the University's main campus. Twenty years ago, the university acquired the 100-year-old structure. Today, after extensive renovation, the old brick building is used for the School of Nursing. But due to an agreement with Chester Fisher, the second floor has been pretty much left unchanged, with just minor modifications to house a cafeteria and museum. These modifications weren't enough to dislodge some of the building's more ethereal inhabitants. Doors shut on their own. Papers blow around in a windowless office. People are heard screaming in the museum after hours.

One morning, the building manager was preparing the building for another day of higher learning. When she attempted to turn on the lights, she felt an icy brush of breath on her wrist. An unseen individual said, "Leave it off." The ghost allowed the switch to operate the lights only after several tries. This so unnerved the building manager that she asked for assistance from a higher plane. A week later, priests from the university blessed the cafeteria and all who worked there. No one has seen the spirit since, and no one yet knows where it has gone.

Another modification to the building was the addition of an overhead walkway across Forbes Avenue to the main campus. I have been there and I know that the walkway was needed. Trying to cross Forbes Avenue at street level during daylight hours is a death-defying dash of the extremely brave or foolhardy. Some students entering that walkway from Fisher Hall find the door being held open for them by a kindly old gentleman. When they turn to thank him for his assistance, he has vanished.

***

Another couple of blocks along Forbes Avenue and we're at Mercy Hospital.

Ed Kelemen

Mercy Hospital

1400 Locust Street
Pittsburgh

The historical marker in front of the hospital says, "Founded in 1847 by the Sisters of Mercy as Pittsburgh's first hospital. Medical internships began in 1848, and the nursing school in 1893. This was the first Mercy hospital worldwide, caring for all patients, especially the community's poor." That says it all.

The Sisters of Mercy never cared about a patient's social or financial history. All were welcomed through its doors. In 1931, during the depths of the Great Depression, donations to keep the hospital running were at a low ebb. Nevertheless, at a time when hospital charges were $4 per day, Mercy Hospital donated $600,000 worth of health care services to those who couldn't pay. Thirty years later when urban blight caused a mass exodus of businesses and services to the suburbs, Mercy Hospital remained and rebuilt, continuing to serve the people of the community.

This community dedication was extended to individual patients. The Sisters of Mercy did everything possible to make each person's stay a comfortable, pleasing, and healing experience.

The oldest building in the complex is part of the original Divine Mercy Hospital. Until the mid-1960s the sixth floor housed the obstetrics ward, where six generations of Pittsburghers were born. Mothers and babies alike benefited from the caring hands of the Sisters of Mercy. My own youngest son, who decided to arrive a bit early on this earth at 3 pounds, 4 ounces, was a beneficiary of Mercy Hospital's neonatal intensive care unit.

Sister Mary Loretta extended her own brand of gentle caring to patients on that ward during her life and seems to have continued her mission past the grave. Sometimes, even the best-intentioned patient care falls a tiny bit short. Nothing important or health threatening, but once in a while, a patient feels a bit of a chill or is slightly parched.

Imagine being in that position. Then, as though your mind is being read, a smiling gray-haired nun shows up at your bed and tucks a warmed blanket around you or brings a sip of ice water to you. This is the thoughtful kindness that sticks with you. Then morning arrives and the ward starts bustling with nurses, doctors, aides, volunteers, food service workers, and everyone else that makes the hospital run smoothly.

Countless patients have complimented the staff for the compassionate nun who brought them that warm blanket or sip of water during the night. They are informed that it has been many years since nuns were part of the treatment staff at this hospital, but just maybe their needs were seen to by the caring ghost of Sister Mary Loretta.

*＊＊

Let's leave the patients of Mercy Hospital to the care of the spectral sister while we continue on eastward along Forbes Avenue for about a mile and a half. Shortly after we pass the Birmingham Bridge on our right, the road swings to the left and starts to rise. At the top of that rise on our right is Craft Avenue, the home of the Pittsburgh Playhouse.

Pennsylvania's Haunted Route 30

The Pittsburgh Playhouse

222 Craft Avenue
Pittsburgh

So far the haunts have been relatively benign, showing themselves here and there, getting glasses of water for bedridden patients, and softly moaning in basements. But theater people tend to be more flamboyant than the average mortal, and their spectral counterparts follow suit.

The Pittsburgh Playhouse, which is Point Park University's performing arts center, has gone through a number of incarnations since it opened in 1933 as Pittsburgh Summer Playhouse. Before that, the buildings on the site included a house of worship, a house of ill repute, a couple of row houses, a restaurant, and a bar. Notable Broadway and Hollywood performers who were trained on its stages include Gene Kelly, Shirley Jones, Sada Thompson, Barbara Feldon, and George Peppard.

A young man by the name of John Johns started a long career as an actor at the Playhouse the year it opened. He would appear in over 75 major productions at the Playhouse during his lifetime. And he has returned for a large number of curtain calls since his death. An accomplished character actor during his life, he continues to be a character afterward. In his obituary on August 9, 1963, *Pittsburgh Press* reporter Henry Ward wrote that Mr. Johns had confided in him his wish to die in the harness as an actor. His wish nearly came true. He suffered a heart attack while emceeing an event in the restaurant and collapsed. A group of acquaintances carried him to Dressing Room 7 to recline while awaiting ambulance. He passed away as he was carried across the threshold of the room. Since then, people hear footsteps climbing the stairs that stop at the door of Dressing Room 7. The footsteps never enter the room and never go back down the stairs. They just end at the door.

A man in formal wear (once called a cutaway or morning suit), is seen walking about backstage from time to time, checking rigging, sets, and props. People who saw him say he looks very like Mr. Johns. The wife of a stage manager encountered a gentleman sitting alone in the theater. Attempts to converse with him failed. Later, when looking over some archival pictures of the theater, she said her uncommunicative neighbor was John Johns.

Another time, at the Hamlet Street Theater, a young actress tied the knot with her loving fiancé at the church on the grounds. During the wedding reception in the lobby of the theater, the poor girl found that her brand-new husband was unfaithful. Not only that, but he was having an affair with a lady of the night who was employed at the brothel on the grounds. Whoever cast this stone into her life managed to kill three birds. The newlywed procured a pistol that wasn't a prop, shot her husband dead, and went upstairs to find his lover. The new widow woman then killed her husband's paramour. Another flight of steps and she was at the balcony. She jumped to her death. This Lady in White still walks the balcony, holding the gun.

After some time had passed, the theater hired a new technical director in charge of rigging and lighting. One day he was in the upper reaches of the theater making adjustments to the lighting. He looked up and observed a woman wearing a white dress with her back towards him. He may or may not have said something to her. In any case, she turned around and raised a gun in his direction. He let his feet do the talking as he left both the theater and his job... Quickly.

An actor once took a break from rehearsal on one of the other stages and entered the Hamlet Street Theater for some solitude and a bit of a rest. He got neither. Looking at the bare stage, he saw an elegant man dressed in a black tuxedo dancing with a young woman wearing a white gown. Thinking another show was in rehearsal, he slid onto a seat to watch. After getting settled, he returned his attention to the stage just in time to watch the pair dissolve before his very eyes. Some of the wags at the theater said that John Johns must have found a friend in the Lady in White. Their afterlife seems to be looking up.

There are many row houses in Pittsburgh. People who have indulged in gentrifying the city's older neighborhoods call them townhouses, but working folk still call them row houses. The Playhouse acquired a bunch of them when it bought the surrounding property. Some of them were still occupied. The vacant ones were used as dressing rooms. Row houses are notorious for fires; when one unit burns, it takes the entire row with it. One night a fire engulfed the dressing rooms. It ignited the adjoining units and the entire row burned. All of the occupants escaped unscathed except a woman named Eleanor and her baby. They perished in the conflagration. Now, late at night she is heard crying for her lost child in one of the dressing rooms. But when the door is opened, nobody is inside. This haunt is called Weeping Eleanor.

Another haunt of the Playhouse has been dubbed Gorgeous George because he is anything but. A tap on the window of the costume shop gets the attention of those inside. They are greeted by a horrible, green, decaying face grimacing in the window. He fades from sight as they watch. More than once this has been mistaken for some sort of theatrical special effect. It isn't.

On Halloween night 1974, a seance was held on the stage of the Rockwell Theater at the Playhouse. The people who were involved in this seance swear that no mind-altering substances were present that evening, not even alcohol. After a while, an apparition coalesced upstage (toward the back of the stage.) It was a man dressed all in red with a worried countenance. He paced from stage right to stage left and back again, his speed increasing. Then he suddenly levitated and began bouncing off the walls, ceiling, and floor, going faster and faster. This performance was interrupted by the ringing of every telephone in the building. One of the five participants in the seance was facing away from the stage towards the seating area. As the peal of the telephones faded, a look of abject terror took over her face. The other four turned around in their seats and were confronted by a full house composed entirely of people wearing clothing of a style popular in the late 1800s and early 1900s. The seance was called off by mutual agreement, and everyone rapidly exited the theater. This haunt has been given the appellation of the Red Bouncing Meanie. As far as I have been able to find out, he never made an encore.

Let's leave these not-so-happy spirits to their digs and get back out in the sunlight.

**

Back on Forbes Avenue, we carefully wend our way through the heart of Pittsburgh's college and medical center. Since jaywalking is a community sport here, we'll keep our eyes peeled for wayward pedestrians. After a few more blocks, there is no way you can miss the imposing edifice on your left known as the Cathedral of Learning at the University of Pittsburgh.

Ed Kelemen

The Cathedral of Learning

University of Pittsburgh

4200 Fifth Avenue
Pittsburgh

In 1921, John G. Bowman, chancellor of the University of Pittsburgh, had a dream. He wanted a towering structure that could be seen for miles in every direction. It would be a symbol of the character of

Pittsburgh and its academic achievements. So that the people of the city would have a sense of ownership in the building, Chancellor Bowman initiated a program called "Buy a brick for Pitt." Each schoolchild who sent in a dime along with a letter explaining how that dime was earned received a certificate for one brick. A total of 97,000 certificates were issued. Pittsburgh industrialists and bankers aided in the procurement of land and the construction.

When it was dedicated in 1937, the Cathedral of Learning at 40 stories was the tallest educational building in the world. It is still the tallest educational building in the Western Hemisphere. Only Moscow State University's main building and two educational buildings in Japan surpass it.

Chancellor Bowman had an idea that got all the disparate communities and neighborhoods of Pittsburgh involved in completing the Cathedral. He got each ethnic group that had a substantial presence in the city to fund, design, and construct a Nationality Room. Each room reflects the customs, history, and lifestyle of the nationality that sponsored it. There are currently 27 nationality rooms, with plans for more. During the school year they are used as classrooms. On weekends and between trimesters, tours are conducted by a student group called Quo Vadis. Self-guided tours are available as well. For more information, call (412) 624-6000 or visit www.nationalityrooms.pitt.edu.

No doubt about it, the Early American Nationality Room is haunted. A wedding quilt that was donated by a relative of Edgar Allan Poe's gets rumpled as though someone sleeps in the bed it covers. The pillow is compressed where a head would lie in repose. The smell of freshly baked bread wafts throughout the room during tours, and a baby cradle that is out of reach gently rocks, unaided. A psychic has seen a woman with her hair pulled back in a bun and a custodian has witnessed a shadow being of some sort in the room. Poltergeist activity has taken place there. Decorations have been struck from their moorings, and well-padded picture frames put away for protection and restoration have been cracked.

Mary Croghan Schenley, who in 1889, donated 300 acres of Schenley Park to the city of Pittsburgh, likes to roam the Nationality Rooms. She shook up Pittsburgh society when at the tender age of 15 she eloped with 43-year-old Captain Edward Schenley. Today he would have to register as a sex offender. During the night hours, Mary rearranges things to suit her. She has a particular affinity for the ballroom, which is made of two rooms transported in their entirety from her childhood home, the Croghan Mansion.

The top floor of this landmark is haunted by unknown spirits, possibly despondent underclassmen waiting for test results.

Bruce Hall is part of the University's Schenley Quadrangle. Although its address is 3990 Fifth Avenue, it actually fronts on Forbes Avenue. Oral tradition in this hotel cum dormitory has it that both the wife and the mistress of the owner of the Schenley Hotel committed suicide in room 1201. One of them is supposed to have hanged herself there; the other jumped to her death. One of this pair has decided to remain and makes her presence known forcefully. So forcefully that Student Housing's Office of Special Events has named her Harriet, even though they have no idea which of them it is. However, they are so convinced of Harriet's presence that they hang a Christmas stocking for her every year.

***

Turn your head to the right and you will see the complex of the Carnegie Library and Museum. If you're wondering whatever became of the thousands of cubic yards of earth, stone, and fill removed from downtown Pittsburgh to make way for building expansion, look no farther. Up to and under the Schenley Quadrangle was an offshoot of Panther Hollow called Saint Pierre's Ravine, crossed by a bridge called the Bellefield Bridge. The only remnant of that bridge is South Bellefield Avenue, which terminates at Forbes Avenue. The bridge however, is not gone. It is still right where it was built, unmolested except for being buried under what was originally the Hump in downtown Pittsburgh.

Ed Kelemen

Carnegie Library and Museum

4400 Forbes Avenue
Pittsburgh

Remember how all those museum movies involve mummies, dinosaurs that have returned to life, and ancient curses? Museums are chocked full of artifacts, fossils, and bodies that once pulsed with life but are now lifeless. The fact that Death reigns supreme is what makes them such spooky places. Carnegie Library and Museum is no different. It holds one of the world's greatest collections of dinosaurs. Its Pharaonic Egyptian display is second to none. And it contains the remains of many people indigenous to this area going back nearly

3,000 years.

Small wonder that employees who work the overnight shift tread the marble floors with trepidation. Is that a footstep the night watchman hears, or just an echo of his own orthopedic soles pacing through the exhibits? Walking through the exhibits of precious metals, gemstones, and jewelry, the guard hears nothing from the state-of-the-art alarm system. But what was that furtive movement over there near the display of diamonds? Was it a ghost or a jewel thief? This question must be answered quickly. Millions of dollars are at stake.

Hollywood movies notwithstanding, this place is haunted inside and out. When the library was built, a cemetery was relocated. Some of the occupants have refused to leave. Academics and other strollers around the grounds and lanes after dark have encountered the spirits of these people dressed in their finest to pass on to the next life. Only they haven't passed on, maybe because their rest was disturbed when their resting place was usurped. No one knows for sure why they're still here. They refuse to answer when spoken to.

Possibly the most famous diorama in the museum is the "Arab Courier Attacked by Lions." A man is being pulled from his camel by a huge African lion. The lion's mate, killed by the man, lies at the camel's feet. The camel extends his throat as far as it will go while his mouth strains wide open in a scream that is never heard. Except at night after all the museum patrons have departed. That's when the faint dying scream of the camel is heard, accompanied by the low guttural growl of the lion as he slashes with talon and teeth.

Inside the building, these denizens give conniptions to those poor souls working the overnight shift. Shades, specters, and shadows are frequently seen throughout the labyrinths, and the people who see them have to decide whether what they are seeing is flesh and blood or something less. The city police lack a sense of humor when it comes to false alarms.

***

About a half mile farther along, old Route 30 leaves Forbes Avenue and bears left onto Beeler Street. Five more blocks and Beeler Street feeds you right onto Wilkins Avenue. Six blocks along Wilkins, if you look closely, you will see Woodland Road lurking off to your left. If you turn onto Woodland, and if the paranoid campus security of this exclusive private university doesn't turn you away, you will find yourself in a beautiful bucolic setting in the midst of the city.

Pennsylvania's Haunted Route 30
Chatham University

1400 Woodland Road
Pittsburgh

Don't let looks cause you to lower your guard. This scenic place is haunted by the ghost of one of the richest men ever to walk the streets of Pittsburgh, Andrew Mellon. In the lower levels of the Mellon Building are a swimming pool and a bowling alley. Andrew Mellon haunts the bowling alley. Maybe he wants to convert a seven-ten pin split before he rests. When he is there, the room turns frigid. People using the bowling alley bring out his wrath. He displays his irritation by causing the pins to reset themselves after they've been knocked down. A 300 game is unlikely event at this alley.

Until 1986, Mr. Mellon had members of the Benedum family to keep him company. Benedum Hall, also called Graystone, was the home of the fabulously rich oilman Michael Benedum and his wife, Sarah. Their son, Claude, fell in love with the family maid, a young woman of no consequence in his parents' estimation. To nip this crush in the bud, Michael and Sarah forced Claude to join the army. World War I was going on at the time. Claude died of pneumonia while in uniform in 1918. The object of his affection soon pined away, and the two of them achieved in the afterlife what they were denied in this one: each other's companionship. When this building was used as a dorm, students said they could hear the pair of them canoodling throughout the house. Claude was also known as a prankster who would pull the covers off sleeping students when the weather was a bit bracing.

The senior Benedum, Michael also had an eye for the hired help. Supposedly he was responsible for getting a maid from a nearby mansion in the family way. Sarah would have none of this. Enraged, she supposedly hanged the maid from the chandelier. From time to time students see the maid hanging from the chandelier still in her black uniform.

Unfortunately, the University sold Benedum Hall in 1986 and a cluster of high-end condos now sit where it once held sway. The ghosts seem to have gone the way of the mansion.

Berry Hall, once a dorm, is now the admissions office. Before coming under the aegis of the university, it was a private residence built in 1895. When it was a dorm, students could hear children crying but could find no children in the building. Most people figure the sounds are made by children who died in the house before it became part of the university.

The lights in the gym have a life of their own. They tend to stay on even after you've turned them off. It is unknown what otherworldly assistance keeps them on.

Laughlin House, formerly the residence of one of the founders of Jones & Laughlin Steel, is the scariest place on campus, even though no ghosts have ever actually been seen. The spirits in residence amuse themselves by opening and closing doors, slamming windows shut, turning various electrical devices on and off, and rearranging students' clothing and other possessions.

The Rea House, built at the same time as the Laughlin House (1912), exhibits some of the mischievous activity associated with poltergeists. Crying babies are sometimes heard, and an unidentified woman's ghost will unsettle you by walking through the front windows.

The Blue Lady of Woodland Hall "lives" in her namesake building. Students wake up with her specter hovering in the air over them. The ghost of a youngster also inhabits the building, looking for someone to join him in play.

With all these haunts compressed into such a small area, it's a wonder that anyone can study.

Ed Kelemen

**

After passing Woodland Road on your left, turn left onto Shady Avenue. When you come to the Pittsburgh Center for the Arts on the right, turn right onto Fifth Avenue. Turn right again at the second traffic signal and you will find yourself on Penn Avenue. At the intersection with Homewood Avenue, you will find Clayton, the fabled home of Henry Clay Frick.

Pennsylvania's Haunted Route 30

The Frick Art and Historical Center

7227 Reynolds Street
Pittsburgh

Few men have been as admired and as vilified during and after their lives as Henry Clay Frick. He was an industrialist, a millionaire, an art patron, and a loving father and husband. Henry Clay Frick was the embodiment of the robber baron. He was blamed for the Homestead Massacre on July 6, 1892. This battle at the Homestead Works of the Carnegie Steel Company left 16 dead and many more wounded. Troops had to be called out to quell the riots that resulted from his heavy-handed way of trying to settle the strike. For the rest of Frick's life the blame for this loss of life hung about his shoulders like an albatross. It was his own private haunt.

He was born at his grandfather's place, called West Overton, just outside of Scottdale, Pennsylvania. As he grew to manhood, he learned the principle of "vertical integration" from his grandfather, Abraham Overholt, who operated a distillery. A vertically integrated manufacturer controls all aspects of the manufacturing process, from raw materials to finished product. Frick saw how this could be applied to the steel Industry. By the time he was 30 years of age he was a multimillionaire (at a time when that actually meant something). He partnered with Andrew Carnegie at 32. Together they owned the largest producer of steel in the entire world, Carnegie Steel. They were just about the richest men in the world at the time.

Frick left a slew of ghosts in his wake. West Overton, where he spent his early years, is one of the most haunted places in Westmoreland County. The home of Old Overholt and Pennsylvania Rye whiskeys is actually a cluster of buildings. It includes the distillery building, the Overholt Mansion, and about a dozen other structures in various states of restoration. The buildings and grounds are haunted by mischievous entities that like to turn lights on and off, knock hats from heads and cameras out of hands, and rattle chains and implements in the barns. Clyde Overholt, who committed suicide with a shotgun, makes his appearance in an upper-story window of the mansion. Another, unknown member of the Overholt clan was found hanging from one of the trees on the grounds. He makes his appearance in that manner to this day. The lady in blue wanders the grounds, and people are heard in the coke ovens, even when the area is deserted.

Henry Clay Frick was the founder of the Southfork Fishing and Hunting Club. The failure of the club's earthen dam on May 31, 1889, resulted in the Johnstown Flood and a tremendous loss of life. This single event is responsible for dozens of hauntings in the Johnstown-St. Michaels area, along the path of the Little Conemaugh River.

Small wonder then that Clayton, where Frick made a home for himself and his family is so haunted that the ghosts have to jostle one another for room. Although the building's address is Reynolds Avenue, the great dowager overlooks Penn Avenue, which is the western end of the Penn-Lincoln Highway. This part of Penn Avenue was the original Route 30 corridor through Pittsburgh and its eastern suburbs.

Martha Frick, the second of his four children, was the absolute light of Henry's life. Maybe it was the contrast between her childlike innocence and the everyday dirty dealings of his life that provided a safe haven from the hatred that he had to endure. He doted on her and gave her everything that one of the richest men in the world could give.

In early August 1891, one week before her sixth birthday, she ingested a pin. The resulting infection killed her. Maybe her wish to bring a bit of happiness to this mansion that has seen so much tragedy is what keeps her coming back. She flits through the vegetation surrounding the mansion, apparently playing a game of tag.

In 1892, in the midst of the Homestead Steel Strike, Henry Clay Frick, Jr. was born. The family hoped that his birth would alleviate some of the pain and suffering that hovered over the family, but it was not to be so. Henry's namesake died in infancy, leaving the family heartbroken again.

One of the things that Henry Clay Frick built for his children was a full-size fabulous playhouse. It was so opulent that it even included a bowling alley. Though it was built some years after her death, Martha Frick must enjoy its amenities. Children are often heard squealing with delight when no one is there.

In the expanded Carriage House is Frick's collection of automobiles and carriages. Tour followers aren't the only ones to visit here. Apparitions in period dress also wander the exhibition, no doubt approving of the millionaire's taste in transportation.

Adelaide Howard Childs Frick, Henry's wife and the mother of this star-crossed family never got over the death of her young children. She left this mortal coil in 1931 but stays on at Clayton. She walks about the mansion, checking to make sure that everything is clean, neat, and in its right place, still overseeing the staff as she did when alive.

In the parlor, otherworldly reflections of the children's funerals appear, with Adelaide Frick in attendance.

***

On this somber note, we depart the City of Pittsburgh, staying on Penn Avenue through the Borough of Wilkinsburg. Penn Avenue will feed us right onto Ardmore Boulevard. As we pass under Interstate Highway I-376, historic Route 30 and modern Route 30 share the same road for a few dozen miles. Along this stretch, US Route 30 gains the appellation Penn Lincoln

Highway, which it will have off and on for the next 300 miles.

Traveling eastward on Route 30, we cross the George Westinghouse Bridge just east of Forest Hills. In 1894, George Westinghouse moved Westinghouse Electric Co. to the hills overlooking the Turtle Creek Valley.

Ed Kelemen

II

In the Suburbs, Exurbs, and Countryside

The George Westinghouse Bridge

Braddock

Almost overnight a little rural hamlet was rushed into the Industrial Age. Factories, subsidiary buildings, homes for the workers, taverns, restaurants, and hotels sprang up like crabgrass. The area was called East Pittsburgh and became a warren of congested and narrow streets, winding lanes, and alleys. The only way into the valley was via the dangerous, twisting Turtle Creek Hill, which boasted an incline of 9 percent. An engineering report in 1931 estimated that the bridge would save travelers at least 30 minutes transiting the Turtle Creek Valley.

Originally the bridge was to be called the New Lincoln Highway Bridge. In January 1931, Westinghouse Electric and Manufacturing Company executives "suggested" that it be named the George Westinghouse Bridge. As the old saying goes, "Money talks and b.s. walks." The longest concrete arch span in the United States was subject to a name change before it was even built.

Shortly after its dedication ceremony in September of 1932, the bridge was carrying 8,000 vehicles per hour. As its popularity soared with motorists happy to eliminate 30 minutes from their eastbound or westbound trips across the gorge, so also did its popularity soar with those unfortunates who opted to end their lives with the four-and-one-half second plunge from the 200-foot tall center span. Since suicide by jumping off a bridge is usually a spur-of-the-moment decision, a chain-link fence along the sidewalks of the bridge brought such deaths to a halt. But not before the following happened:

In 1957, a member of the clergy, Father E., was driving across the bridge when a car came to an abrupt stop in front of him. The driver jumped out, ran around the car, and dived over the handrail.

Father E. ran to the spot and looked down to see where the person had landed. He could see nothing. He spent a few quiet moments there praying for the tortured soul who saw this as the only way to solve his problems. When he turned back to face the roadway, the car had disappeared as well. Fearing ridicule, the priest shared this event only with his close relatives, and then only after the exact same thing happened to his brother-in-law years later. When his brother-in-law witnessed it, the car didn't disappear and there was a shattered body lying on the ground beneath the bridge. The brother-in-law was my dad.

The first person to die in a plummet from this bridge was a construction worker who tumbled from a beam in 1931. From time to time people see a man teetering on the edge of the understructure of the bridge. It seems to be the ghost of the man who fell accidentally because, in the bridge's entire history, only one rescue was performed. It was of two young children who had managed to climb one of the arches. Nobody is on record as witnessing any of the other falls or jumps from this bridge. The only evidence is broken bodies on the banks of the shallow Turtle Creek.

***

If you look to your right as you cross this bridge, again traveling east, you can catch a glimpse of the Edgar Thompson Steelworks. The site of this factory is haunted by the ghosts of British soldiers who were massacred by the French and Indians during General Braddock's campaign of 1755. George Washington, a young man at the time, observed many of these phantasms himself when he organized a retreat of the survivors. He often returns to supervise the evacuation of those soldiers.

We'll head east along Route 30 for just about 5-3/4 miles. Then we'll take a left onto Leger Road and go one and one-third miles to Old Brush Creek Cemetery.

Pennsylvania's Haunted Route 30
Old Brush Creek Cemetery
Ardara

Overgrown and neglected tombstones supporting each other.

The graves in this venerable old cemetery date back to the 1700s and continue to the mid-1900s. Today it looks like a Hollywood set for a movie about hauntings. The gravestones are crooked, leaning, and falling over. The ancient metal fence is down in most places and held up by stones, logs, and vegetation in others. Speaking of vegetation, the only plants visible are those provided by nature. That is a gentle way of putting it. In fact, the cemetery is weed choked.

A respectful stroll indicates that it was not always such. The graves themselves are in neat, orderly rows. The marking stones and monuments are of first-class stonework. Veterans of every war from the

Revolutionary War to World War II are resting here.

What happened?

Local lore has it that a massacre of Native Americans, Indians if you will, took place nearby. Imagine how you would feel facing a strangely dressed race of people equipped with instruments of war you never dreamed of. The Native Americans massacred here by English settlers must have felt the way you or I would feel if aliens from outer space arrived and exterminated humans simply to take over the ground on which we stood. For that is the reason that the massacre took place – to acquire land.

The story goes that it was a settlement of Choctaw Indians that was eradicated, but the nearest the Choctaw Indians ever came to Western Pennsylvania was over 500 miles away. Possibly it was a group of Chippewa or Shawnee Indians.

In any case, it is no surprise that the spirits of these outgunned residents refuse to depart. The European settlers may have evicted the corporeal bodies of those who came first, but their ghosts are impervious to bullets.

People walking the grounds of this old graveyard hear footsteps in the grass shadowing their every move. Faint images of entities are seen flitting from tree to tree in the shadows.

For more than 200 years, this graveyard has been left unmolested. Supposedly, the apparitions on these grounds were first seen after an Indian burial ground nearby was disturbed so that a gas well could be drilled – another unceremonious eviction to acquire land. One explanation I've heard is that the Indians are desecrating this cemetery as revenge for the destruction of their own. This, I feel, is wrong. I don't think that the spirituality of

Native Americans would permit them to cause the desecration of any culture's burial place.

Most likely, they stand aside and watch with amusement as the descendants of those responsible for their extermination cause the vandalism to the burial place of their own ancestors.

***

Right about here, we enter Westmoreland County. The Lincoln Highway Heritage Corridor begins at the county line and extends along the original path of Route 30 for 200 miles.

Up the hill from the graveyard we'll get back onto Route 30 and continue heading east. We'll travel past Norwin and Irwin, where there's an entrance to the Pennsylvania Turnpike for those who like to zoom by haunts at 65 miles per hour.

The rest of us will continue along Route 30, passing Jeannette and a bunch of strip malls and shopping centers before finding ourselves on the Greensburg bypass, where the road abruptly changes from a four-lane highway studded with businesses and traffic signals to a limited-access road with spaced exits. We will take one of those exits, the one for Pittsburgh Street, which just happens to be the way Old Route 30 went. When we come to PA Route 130, we'll travel west on it for a short while.

As we come out of the underpass, on the left is Seton Hill University.

Ed Kelemen

Seton Hill University
Greensburg

In 1918, as World War I came to an end, the Catholic Sisters of Charity opened a small liberal arts college for women in Greensburg. Since that time it has grown into a moderate-size coeducational university with several thousand students, and the buildings and grounds have become populated with their share of ghostly presences.

In the Administration building, which was once the mother house, people hear the pounding of fists on wood late at night. A rather apocryphal tale has it that, in the early twentieth century, an elderly nun fell asleep in the basement. Supposedly a custodian saw her lying there and assumed that she was dead. She was buried alive. She awakened in her coffin and beat on the lid until she died for real. It is her spirit pounding in the late hours in the Administration Building.

I have been told that I am an unusually sound sleeper, having slept through the sounds of thunderstorms, passing railroad trains, and even a vehicle accident outside my bedroom window. But even if this elderly nun was twice as sound a sleeper as I am, she probably would have awakened when the undertaker inserted a large needle into her femoral artery to replace her blood with embalming fluid.

The late-night sounds at the Administration Building may be of otherworldly origin, but they are probably not generated by a prematurely buried nun.

The spirits of teaching nuns long deceased walk from one classroom to another in the labyrinthine corridors of Maura Hall. If you meet up with one of them, don't bother to ask for directions. She won't answer you.

Brownlee Residence is a dorm for freshman women, and some of the young ladies report that their sleep is disturbed at night by someone running up and down the hallway on the first floor. When a resident opens her door to investigate or remonstrate, no one is ever there, even as the sounds continue. One of the first-floor dorm rooms has a mysterious purple light in the corner of the room. The shadow of a girl who hanged herself many years ago is said to be imprinted on the hall wall across from the room where she ended her life. A ghost of a priest hurries across the main parking lot heading in the general direction of the Administration Building. Possibly he is heading for St. Joseph's Chapel, late for vespers.

Speaking of St. Joseph's Chapel, a ghostly nun has been seen in the room directly to the right of the organ. The organ door opens and closes, seemingly on its own, and ghostly hymns waft in the still air of the chapel as an unseen chorus sings.

On foggy evenings and the predawn hours, a woman stops traffic on the main driveway. When a driver stops the car for her, she fades into the fog.

A little boy plays with a ball nearby on the grass. When disturbed he gathers up his ball and runs into oblivion, screaming all the while as though being chased.

Indistinct shapes wander the sisters' cemetery, hovering over the graves.

***

Let's travel back through the underpass and follow PA Route 130 (which follows Old Route 30) when we turn left at the second traffic signal. Two blocks later, turn left on Main Street. At the next traffic light, look to the left and see the Westmoreland County Courthouse.

Westmoreland County Courthouse Square
Greensburg

The Courthouse

The current Westmoreland County Courthouse, with its domed roof flying a gigantic flag of the United States, is the first thing you see when approaching Greensburg from any direction. It was built on the site of three previous buildings and opened for business in 1906.

The haunting takes place on the upper level of the parking garage next door. The garage was erected on the site of the old county jail, which had been in use from the early 1900s until the 1960s. During its early days, many prisoners convicted of capital offenses exited this mortal life at the end of a sturdy hemp rope right there. Just think of the emotions that permeate this area.

During the 1980s, the 911 Dispatch Center was located on the premises. The 911 Center was also the location of all the security monitors for the Courthouse Complex. One evening in 1984, the dispatch operators were stunned to see the lower torso of a person hanging in the hallway leading from the magistrate's office to the parking garage.

Of course the 911 dispatch operators dispatched someone immediately to investigate a suicide in progress. They ran to that location. Nothing looked amiss, but they did encounter a chillingly cold area. They were actually observed on the monitors in the 911 center passing through the hanging body.

Research by the Westmoreland County Historical Society revealed that the spot where the body was observed on the monitor correlated to the second floor of the old county jail, where the early hangings took place. Could it be that one of those prisoners from a hundred years ago liked the place so much that he decided to hang around?

The exact location of this haunting is where the pedestrian bridge from the parking garage meets the courthouse building. Many people, including me, have experienced a chill when walking through the spot where people have met their maker against their will.

The security camera is located where the pedestrian bridge meets the building

***

How are we going to get back on 30 heading the right way? Easy! Go to the next traffic light, turn left, go one block, and turn left again. Now we're back on PA Route 130. Follow it through Greensburg until Pittsburgh Street turns to the right. Continue straight until the road leads right back onto present-day Route 30.

Pass Westmoreland Mall, the strip malls, and the fast-food places. A few miles down the road on your right is the entrance to St. Xavier Convent and School.

Ed Kelemen

St. Xavier Convent and School

Latrobe

The following incident is best described by the person who experienced it, Mary Ann Mogus:

"The field adjacent to St. Xavier's, a former academy for young women, is believed to be the site of Fort Proctor, one of the stockaded forts set up to protect the then western frontier during the French and Indian War (1758-1763). Though records exist of a building on the property owned by Proctor, the actual fort has never been found. In the 1970s, a group of amateur and professional archeologists received permission to search for evidence of this fort.

I've participated in many digs through the years, but this is the only excavation where something truly eerie happened to me. The site had been opened for a month and volunteers came and went according to their schedule. There were several of us supervising. One sunny day everyone had to leave for a bit. I agreed to remain in the field alone until the other excavators returned. The field was open, but bordered by woods to the south as well as a spring that fed into a small stream.

The group had set aside a privy area in the woods. I was working on a section of an excavation but decided that I had to make a pit stop. As I started into the woods, I was overcome with a sense of dark menace. I could not continue into the woods, no matter how much I needed a pit stop. I stood there and waited but the feeling would not go away. Instead it intensified, and I saw a man carrying an old-fashioned musket and dressed in clothing from the eighteenth century. The menace was so overwhelming that I hurried back to the open field and sat waiting until others returned. When the gang started to filter back, the menace evaporated.

No one else at the site had ever felt this before. I have no idea whether the menace was the ghost of some previous occupant who wanted no one there at that time or whether there was something really to fear in those woods and the ghost was a warning.

The site was closed the following year. While the excavators located evidence of eighteenth-century occupation, there was no definitive evidence of a fort at the location."

This must have been one menacing entity to stop M. A. Mogus in her tracks. I know this no-nonsense lady. She once got into such an argument with a ghost at another location, West Overton Museum (the birthplace of Henry Clay Frick), that the ghost followed her orders and stopped messing with the lights. The particular ghost in question was in the distillery building at the Museum. Ms. Mogus had occasion to be there alone and was turning on the lights and heat for others who would arrive later. Each time she turned on the lights in the distillery room, a short time later they would go off. She checked the breaker box and the main switch and found everything copacetic. She returned to the distillery room and turned the lights on again, with the same results. After the third time this happened, she called out, "If these lights don't come back on and stay on, I am going to kick some ghostly butt." The lights came back on and stayed on.

***

Let's mosey on along Route 30. Taking a left at the next traffic light on Route 30 will find us on the grounds of Saint Vincent College.

Pennsylvania's Haunted Route 30

Saint Vincent College

Latrobe

View from PA Route 981

On October 25, 1846, Father Sebastian Wimmer, who took the religious name of Boniface, was accompanied by 18 monks when he opened St. Vincent Monastery and School in Latrobe. Within 10 years, the monastery was populated by over 200 monks.

Today the Pittsburgh Steelers use the school for summer training camp. Thousands of diehard fans flock to the site every summer to watch Steelers practices and scrimmages. Unbeknownst to these hordes of football fans, they are standing elbow to elbow with hordes of denizens from beyond the grave.

The founder, Father Boniface, returns every year on the anniversary of his death, December 8. Ostensibly, he returns for two reasons. He takes a quick tour of the campus to see how the school that he founded has prospered in the year since his last visit. Then he goes to the crypt beneath the basilica and checks on all who have passed before offering mass for the souls of the departed in the basilica. His is a gentle and caring spirit, and a sighting of him is a rite of passage for freshmen students. He has never indicated whether or not he is a Steelers fan and has never been seen wearing black and gold.

The Sauerkraut Tower overlooks the campus up near the Sis and Herman Dupre Science Pavilion Chemistry Building. Its only earthly purpose is to serve as a landmark from times gone by. Its unearthly purpose is to serve as a receptacle for the spirit of an unknown Benedictine monk. You see, in 1893 Brother Wolfgang Traxler built the tower as part of a gravity flow system to move water throughout the campus. Its supposed capacity was 80,000 gallons per day. For half a century, the food at St. Vincent was prepared and served by Benedictine sisters from the town of Eichstatt in Bavaria. Those industrious nuns also made sauerkraut that was famous for its flavor. To keep it cool as it aged, it was stored in the water tower. Eventually the water tower became known as the Sauerkraut Tower.

To feed Pittsburgh's ravenous steel industry, every scrap of coal that could be found was mined throughout Pennsylvania. The area around the university is no different. Like most of Westmoreland County, it is honeycombed with coal mines. The mines caused a shift in the bedrock and, after 50 years, water started disappearing from the system into the mines below. That meant that one of the brothers had to climb the ten flights of stairs three times a day to check the water level.

During the 1930s one unfortunate brother had the bad luck to get part of his loose-fitting habit caught in the machinery of the windmill atop the tower. He was strangled by the ever-tightening cloth around his neck. He still carries out his duties today. You can hear his footfalls on the steps as he trudges to the top of the tower to check the water level. So that he doesn't misstep in his afterlife as he did in bodily form, he turns on the lights inside the empty building. He sometimes gets caught looking out one a window of the tower. Campus security frequently has to turn those lights off and wishes it would dawn on the monk that the university is now hooked into the city water supply – and has been since 1942.

Aurelius Hall houses the Alex G. McKenna School of Business, Economics, and Government, and a few disorderly haunts, and one protective spirit. Years back, before its multimillion-dollar renovation, it was mostly used for student housing.

Youngsters being youngsters, it was inevitable that someone would play with a ouija board sooner or later. Some girls on the sixth floor managed to call up a spirit by the name of Henry in this manner. They passed this information on to a few of their male classmates. In order to show off and to impress the young ladies, these boys took to insulting and agitating the spirit. That was a mistake. Henry started telling their secrets through the Ouija board.

In exasperation, the boys called the spirit out. "Hank," they teased, "If you're so real, give us a sign." He did. The full-length mirror hanging on the wall of their dorm room shot off the wall across the room and shattered against the opposite wall. Their screaming brought out the rest of the residents. When things settled down, the boys returned to their room only to find it permeated with the smell of something rotting. The very next day, through the Ouija board, they made their apologies to Henry, who then left them alone.

Another student, class president at the time, was in the lounge at Aurelius Hall when the television came on of its own accord one night. "It didn't even have a remote control," he said. The same student heard pounding and shuffling on the seventh floor, as though an impromptu basketball game were being played there. But when he climbed the steps to that floor, he found it empty.

Aurelius Hall has also been the home to a spook who liked to walk through a dorm room shuffling his feet. The student who called the room home would find her dresser drawers opened, and lights would flicker on and off by themselves. Rather than being scared, she somehow felt that she was being protected. The ghost even managed to find her lost ring. It dropped out of thin air onto her dresser with a clattering sound.

Gerard Hall's haunts aren't quite as garrulous as the ones of Aurelius Hall. They confine themselves to walking in the hallways and producing cold spots here and there.

Opened in 2002, St. Benedict Hall, used for freshmen housing, is home to the impish ghost of a little girl named Jenny. She likes to appear here and there in the rooms. She gets blamed for little trinkets going missing and hand prints on the outside of the windows.

Every year after midnight mass on Christmas Eve, when the Basilica is deserted and everyone has departed to celebrate the holiday, security personnel hear parishioners still inside. Kneelers strike the floor, music and singing go on, and even incense can be smelled long after it should have dissipated.

The grounds outside the building aren't immune to haunts, either. The adjacent cemetery, where many Benedictine monks and nuns (along with many parishioners) are interred has been the site of more than one ethereal funeral procession. Faces appear above tombstones, only to fade as they are approached. A statue of the Blessed Virgin Mary is said to shed tears of blood whenever someone with a deep sorrow prays to her, and a statue of Mary holding the body of Jesus will look up and acknowledge your presence if you sit long enough on the bench in front of it.

A tree trunk in the cemetery has been whittled into the shape of a high-backed chair or throne. The roots of this tree entwine the grave of a young child who died in the early twentieth century. The ghost of that young boy is seen sitting on that tree throne.

Ghostly nuns from St. Xavier's walk from their convent to the Basilica to attend mass. A monk, face covered in a cowl, walks the fields between St. Xavier's and St. Vincent. If you ever get close enough to see, the cowl is empty and the monk is faceless.

***

Let's head a bit east and visit the headquarters of the Liuncoln Highway Heritage Corridor.

Ed Kelemen

Lincoln Highway Heritage Corridor

Lincoln Highway Experience
3435 State Route 30 East
Latrobe

A few miles east of St. Vincent's Route 30 enters the Loyalhanna Gorge, a beautiful wooded cut that has been carved out by the Loyalhanna Creek over the mellennia. The eastbound lanes run along the southern bank while the westbound lanes run on the northern bank. Right where the road enters the gorge you will see a stone mansion on the right positioned as though it is guarding the entrance to the gorge.

A nearby historical marker identifies it as the Johnston House, built in 1815 by Alexander Johnston, the father of William F. Johnston who was governor of

Pennsylvania from 1848 to 1852. The elder Johnston built it to be close to the Kingston Works, his nearby iron works consisting of a forge, rolling mill, and so forth. It was first known as the Kingston House. Later, after realizing that the iron works were never going to be profitable, the building served as public inn while the future governor of the state was growing up. Eventually, it became known as the Johnston House.

During the two centuries of its existence, the Johnston House has experienced and hosted all sorts of emotionally-charged events from births to weddings to deaths. It's a small wonder then that some of the people who have passed through its doors in life have lingered on after their death.

In 2012, the Lincoln Highway Experience, a museum dedicated to the preservation of the memory of the Lincoln Highway opened within the walls of the Johnston House, which had been recently purchased by the Lincoln Highway Heritage Corridor organization. Museum director Olga Herbert oversaw the installation of historic artifacts connected with the famous road that include a pair of restored and working early 20th century gasoline pumps, place settings from the world-famous Grand View Ship Hotel, and photographs that prevent such attractions as the Coffee Pot Restaurant in Bedford from being only dim memories. All this is accompanied by its award-winning 13-minute film, "Through the Windshield," that celebrates the rich history of the nation's first coast-to-coast highway.

Shortly after it's grand opening, staff and visitors alike became aware that they weren't the only inhabitants of the Johnston House. Strange sounds and barely seen movements were reported to the museum director. Olga

Herbert took matters under advisement and made arrangements for a paranormal investigation to be conducted on the premises.

So, in early Summer of 2012, Dr. Laurel J. Black and members of Ghost Researcher in Pennsylvania conducted an in-depth paranormal investigation of the venerable old building. In addition to members who are sensitive to the presence of paranormal activity, the group used digital tape recorders to acquire EVPs (Electronic Voice Phenomena) and K2 Meters to detect electromagnetic field fluctuations. Digital cameras were also in their arsenal. As a result of their investigation, they reported the appearance of at least four different spectral entities residing in the house.

One is an elderly woman wearing clothing reminiscent of that of the mid-1800s. She sits quietly in a rocking chair in what is now the museum office, gazing pensively out the adjacent window, surrounded by an aura of sadness. She seems to be caught in a time loop and all attempts to communicate with her have been futile.

Another is a little tow headed little boy wearing a blue suit, shorts, and long white stockings who peeks around doorways at adults, then runs away down the hall when he is observed.

The museum gift shop is home to another female spirit who perhaps likes to browse the books and artifacts for sale there while the fourth spirit is a man prefers to remain in the third floor attic.

An EVP was presented of a person whispering "Who?" Another EVP of a loud bang was also played back by the group.

Stop in. Who knows who else you may meet here at

this former stagecoach stop located near the location of one of the early highway's first toll houses. And, that lady peering over your shoulder as you examine items in the museum's gift shop just might give you some advice on what is the best buy. Pay attention to her, she's been there a long time.

If you are traveling this way in the summer, consider stopping in at Idlewild Amusement Park, independently rated the best family-oriented amusement park in the country. There is no better place for a picnic. I recommend the smoked turkey legs.

* * *

Passing Idlewild Park on our right brings us to a B&B that was until recently called the Lady of the Lake.

Ed Kelemen

Lady of the Lake

Ligonier

The haunted building as it once appeared.

How about a comfortable overnight stay in a pastoral bed and breakfast that has been enjoyed by people like composer Andre Previn and actress Mia Farrow? For a little icing on the cake, suppose the place is haunted? You're too late. The Lady of the Lake B&B has been closed since its purchase by Ligonier Camp and Conference Center. The lake of the Lady was originally an ice pond operated by the Consolidated Ice Company a century ago. The new owners repaired it and will soon open a day camp offering swimming, boating, and picnicking.

When it was open for business, three buildings were available for rent. If you wished a visit from the gentle spirit at the Lady of the Lake, you chose the main house because she never ventured into any of the other buildings. If you were lucky enough to encounter this particular haunt, you wouldn't be spooked. That's because a personal appearance was never made. Your stay would never have been interrupted by shrieks, groans, moans, or glowing protoplasm. The most the Lady ever did was to noisily disturb knickknacks on the first floor while you were comfortably ensconced under the covers in the second-floor bedroom.

As part of the renovations, the houses on the property are being razed. I'm sure the gentle and timid little haunt will vacate the area when it gets too busy for her. Either that, or possibly the little ghost will entertain herself by playing with people's pik-a-nik baskets.

***

Main Street in Ligonier follows the original path of Route 30, so we will, too. An excellent place for lunch is the Ligonier Tavern at 137 West Main right in the heart of town.

Ed Kelemen

The Ligonier Tavern

Ligonier

You may not be eating alone, even if you ask for a table for one. Haunts abound in this longtime eating and drinking establishment. But even if you aren't joined by someone who is lingering awhile on this earthly side, you are guaranteed to enjoy your repast. Built in 1895 by a former mayor of Ligonier, it has been a restaurant more or less continuously since 1927

Jan McLaughlin, a local writer, had an unusual experience while visiting the tavern. She has been kind enough to allow us to quote from the article she wrote:

"My friend Carolyn and I went up the dim stairway to explore the third floor. Other than the murky light from the stairway below, the room was in total darkness. We talked as we felt all around the walls for a light switch. Unable to find one we retreated to the lower floors, taking pictures as we went. We even took a photo of the fireplace in the men's room on the second floor.

We returned to the first floor to the Mellow Mike (a local performing arts group) entertainment. They sing songs they've written, play various instruments, and read poetry of their own creation, harking back to the days of troubadours.

I listened for awhile but felt drawn, somehow, to go back to the third floor. No one would go with me, so I went alone. I reset my camera for night shots. Nothing much could be seen without the flash. After taking many pictures I sat back in the small alcove of the three-sided turret, under the witch's-hat peaked roof.

I can't say I felt a cold spot. I felt peaceful and calm. I heard the music from below but I wasn't drawn to it. And I didn't notice the ghost when I was taking the picture.

Imagine my shock when about two months later, as I was transferring it from my camera to my computer, *I SAW HIM.*

The photo appears to show a person standing at the end of the bar. Knowing I was up there alone, I was intrigued, but I never thought 'ghost.' I assumed ghosts were gauzy images without definite form.

Photo: Apparition on third floor of Ligonier Tavern (Photo used with permission of Jan McLaughlin)

    I told no one about this image. A month or so later, when I returned to Ligonier Tavern to lunch with a friend, I asked the owner if they ever had something sitting on the end of the bar. Perhaps a hanging plant? He said no. Then I asked him to view the picture in my camera. He became excited and said there had been incidents. He had goosebumps and took the picture back to show the employees.

    He stated that when he closes up at night, he starts at the top floor and works his way down. On *several* occasions on the third floor (which hadn't been in use) all the candles were lit. This spooked him so he much he removed all the candles.

    Also, an employee was severely frightened by a ghost she saw on the second floor. The apparition appears to be a Viet Nam era soldier wearing camouflage uniform with pants tucked in but ballooning out over combat boots. I've heard of Green Berets, but my guy has a red beret.

The face is featureless but appears to be looking directly at me. He appears relaxed in my presence."

So, if you happen to be hoisting one or two up at the third-floor bar, raise your glass and toast this lost soldier. Maybe he'll do the same in return.

***

We will leave Ligonier and travel a bit south on PA Route 711 to visit the site of a particularly heinous deed that has caused the curse of the Broken Oak.

Ed Kelemen

The Broken Oak

Stahlstown

Five miles south of Route 30 on PA Route 711 is an ancient shattered oak tree. It is marked by a sign that says, "Broken Oak Road."

During the early 1800s, Indian raids were still a fact of frontier life. Folk who lived in these parts sometimes had a false sense of security since Fort Ligonier was only five miles away. Think about it. In those days when roads were pathways and rapid transit meant horseback, even if you were running for your life, it could take hours to reach the protection of the fort. Compound it with a pair of children barely out of diapers. How long would a couple carrying two kids and a flintlock rifle, looking over their shoulders, all the while trying to be quiet as possible, take to travel five miles?

Small wonder then that most frontier families built their homes like blockhouses. Logs stopped bullets, and rifle ports strategically placed along the walls kept attackers at bay. The natives in this area were neither stupid, nor peaceful. They knew exactly how long it took a farmer to reload his rifle. When they attacked, they were sure to draw his fire. While he was pouring a powder charge, topping it with a wadded lead ball, ramming it home, and finally filling the flash pan with powder, the Indians would rush one or more sides of the home with burning brands. Logs don't stop fire, but sometimes the farmer could hold out until reinforcements came from the fort or neighboring farms. Other times, the reinforcements found only scalped bodies and smoking embers.

This happened here. A local farm couple and their older children held out as long as they could. It wasn't long enough. They were scalped and their bodies left to rot.

For whatever reason, maybe as hostages or as slaves, the two youngest children, a boy and a girl were taken prisoner. At some point along the footpath, they became too much of a burden for the war party. Maybe they couldn't keep pace with their captors. Maybe they were crying. Maybe they froze in terror. Nobody knows.

The two little children were tied to an oak tree and tortured to death. As their screams diminished, they were scalped and left to provide food for scavenging animals.

The forces of nature can be capricious. Local lore has it that, as punishment for being even a small part of this atrocity, the tree was struck by lightning and blasted to splinters some ten feet above the ground, never to grow another leaf. As each tree rots and returns to the earth from which it came, a nearby oak is shattered. All that is left is one branch reaching to the heavens pleading for mercy that never came for the children and will never come for the tree.

Warm summer evenings are the best time to just stop and listen quietly near the tree. That's when you can hear the pleading, whimpering cries of the children as a faint echo on the night breeze.

***

Let's head back north on PA Route 711.Coming back Fort Ligonier will on our right and a Get-Go gasoline station and convenience store on your left where PA Route 711 crosses Route 30.

Pennsylvania's Haunted Route 30

The Lost Soldier of Fort Ligonier

**Get-Go's
Route 30 and Route 711
Ligonier**

Fort Ligonier is an historically-accurate restoration of a British Fort that was erected during the French and Indian War in the late 1750s and served as the launching site of General Forbes' campaign to capture Fort Duquesne at the confluence of the Allegheny and Monongahela Rivers. It was the final link in a chain of forts across Pennsylvania designed to protect travelers and colmmerce along the road from Philadelphia to Pittsburgh. This road later came to be Route 30.

An excellent book about the hauntings of Fort Ligonier was written and published in 2008 by Cassandra Fell and Walter L. Powell titled, "Ghosts and Legends of Fort Ligonier." Mentioned within the covers is the apparition of Phoebe St. Clair who tends to cling to her parlor at the Fort Ligonier Muszeum, as well as others. The book is available for sale at the Fort Ligonier Museum and Shop.

But, now it appears that one of the ghosts has wandered afield, abandoning his milityary post at the fort. Employees and customers alike have observed a gentleman in full French and Indian War military regalia, complete to his rifle walking across the lot of the service station at Get-Gos across the street from the fort. This usually happens in the evening hours and when there are no reenactors in the vicinity. When somene exits the store to ask the fellow what he is up to, he can't be found. He just fades into thin air.

***

OK, we're going to climb Laurel Mountain a few miles eastward, so let's get going in that direction.

Pennsylvania's Haunted Route 30

A Ghost on Laurel Mountain

Early on in our travel across the commonwealth, we had occasion to visit the Old Allegheny County Jail and the Bridge of Sighs. While we were there, I mentioned the ill-fated romance between the warden's wife, Kate Soffell, and Ed Biddle. He had been convicted of a murder during a bungled robbery on Mount Washington (overlooking the city of Pittsburgh). He and his brother Jack, the notorious Biddle Boys, were waiting for the executioner to carry out their sentence. It was 1902.

A couple of years before, Peter Soffel had a summer place built just east of Laughlintown on Route 30, partway up Laurel Mountain. It was for Kate and the children to escape the stifling heat and choking smog that had given Pittsburgh its reputation as the Smoky City. As a summer house, it was more than adequate. It was a handsome, stylish, and sturdy stone building, complete with maid's quarters, a fish pond, and an in-ground pool. Kate no longer got the opportunity to enjoy summers at this residence after she completed her prison sentence.

Diana Hunt wrote in the November 9, 2011, issue of the *Beanery Writers Online* literary magazine that her parents purchased the place. She lived there from 1973 to 1979. One night when she was alone in the house with her dog, a misty human shape materialized in the dining room. It whirled about, then entered the living room, paused, exited through the open French doors, and disappeared. Her dog followed the ghost with his eyes as it promenaded through the house.

Ms. Hunt speculates that the ghost just might be the shade of Kate Soffel returning to a place where she had found happiness in life.

Ed Kelemen

***

A little ways up the mountain from here, we come to:
Dead Man's Curve

Laurel Mountain

The Infamous Curve

At the end of a long downhill grade heading west from the summit of Laurel Mountain on Route 30 lies a dangerous hairpin curve. Drivers really have no idea how sharply it curves until they find their vehicle struggling to stay on the highway. It starts with a curve to the left, which is immediately followed by a sharp switchback to the right.

Over the decades the curve has achieved a great deal of infamy, especially among the trucking fraternity. A trucker must show care coming down the long descent to avoid burning out the brakes before getting to the curve. The best way to do this is to downshift and allow the engine to maintain the slower speed. This use of the jake brake is announced by a roaring as the engine strains to retard the speed. If the load is heavy enough, the jake brake must be augmented by the air brakes, which heat up and sometimes overheat. When this happens, the only thing holding back the truck is the jake brake, which sometimes just isn't enough.

From the 1940s well into the 1970s, too many trucks lost their brakes and failed to negotiate that curve. The lucky ones who actually made it were faced with another two and a half miles of downhill to further burn their brakes. The little hamlet of Laughlintown at the bottom of the mountain was frequently treated to the sight and sound of a 40- and 50-ton payload semi roaring through at high speed, with the driver hoping to regain control on the long flat stretch just west of town.

Finally, after numerous fatalities, the PA Department of Transportation lowered the westbound lane of the highway some fifteen feet so that an out-of-control vehicle couldn't change lanes and strike oncoming traffic head-on while attempting to negotiate Dead Man's Curve. While this undoubtedly works, it offers little consolation to drivers who wreck on this curve. Shortly after the improvement was completed, a truck carrying a load of asphalt jackknifed and overturned on the curve. The asphalt ignited, leaving burn marks on the highway that can be seen to this day.

On May 11, 1989, before the improvements were made, a runaway truck that lost its brakes here made it through the hairpin curve. But this only set it up for another long downhill stretch. It was impossible to engage the jake brakes at this speed. The truck careened on down the slope to Laughlintown, brakes burnt out. It smashed into a car and a house before coming to a rest. Five people died, including the truck driver. Just one week later, the scenario was repeated without casualties when the driver steered into a ditch. Both of these trucks successfully negotiated the curve but burned out their brakes doing so. These two accidents provided the final impetus to improve the road.

Improvements consisted of a mandatory rest stop on top of the mountain where truckers can cool their brakes and a runaway ramp on the lower slope. These, along with a plethora of warning signs starting some miles east, have definitely saved lives. But the hapless driver who approaches Dead Man's Curve with fried brakes is still pretty much on his own.

Locals report hearing screaming, roaring engines, brakes, and tearing metal near the curve, even when there isn't a truck in sight.

***

Continue over the top of Laurel Mountain and enjoy the view. If your appetite is big enough, stop in at Walat's just over the crest for one of their legendary sandwiches. And if the server asks you how many potatoes you want for your french fries, better start off with one. Wallatt's slices up some massive Idahoans for an order of fries.

At the bottom of the long downhill grade is the country village of Jennerstown, named for Dr. Edward Jenner, discoverer of the smallpox vaccine. Consider stopping in at Our Coal Miners Cafe or Turillo's Steak House. Our next stop is North Star High School.

Pennsylvania's Haunted Route 30

North Star High School

Boswell

North Star High School in Boswell, PA, is the home of the Cougars football and basketball Teams. It is small when compared to the huge urban and suburban high schools where you can spend four years without meeting all your classmates. At North Star High School, everyone knows everyone.

Stories abound about the varsity wrestling coach. One day he made a misstep at the top of a stairwell. He fell, tumbled, rolled, and bounced down three flights of steps to his death. But he didn't leave the school. Janitors have seen him where he fell. One time, bloody footprints led to the wrestling room, where an equally bloody knife was found. The police were called, the school evacuated, and a thorough search conducted, but nothing was found. The night cleaning staff has also heard mysterious sounds.

Ed Kelemen

This report is from a number of online sources. I have not been able to independently verify any of these claims from any other sources. One of the sources, http://theshadowlands.net/places/pennsylvania.htm, removed reports concerning the haunting at this school as of October 2007. I offer it as a curiosity and an example of how a rumor can get out of control.

Pennsylvania's Haunted Route 30

Flight 93 National Memorial

Stonycreek Township

On September 11, 2001, Ziad Jarrah, and three fellow terrorists boarded United Airlines Flight 93 at Gate 17, Terminal A, Newark International Airport, en route to San Francisco International Airport. They knew something that the other 40 SOBs (Souls On Board) didn't know: the aircraft was never going to reach its destination. They planned to hijack the plane and crash it into either the nation's Capitol building or the White House in Washington, D.C., causing as much loss of life that they could.

They had studied, practiced, and rehearsed their crime over and over, until they each could perform their assigned parts in this tragedy in their sleep. They thought that they had allowed for every possible contingency and obstacle. And they had--all but one. They forgot that they were dealing with freedom-loving, patriotic American citizens. As soon as the passengers aboard Flight 93 learned by cellphones of the other three suicide attacks that morning on the two World Trade Center Towers in New York City and on the Pentagon in Washington, they did what American citizens are expected to do – they took a vote. And they voted to thwart the terrorists' intentions.

The terrorists' plan to crash the plane into a political target came to an abrupt end when passenger Todd Beamer uttered that heroic phrase, "Are you guys ready? Let's roll!" A few minutes later, at eleven one-hundredths of a second after 10:03 a.m., the aircraft disintegrated when it plowed into a quiet pasture in Stonycreek Township, PA at 563 miles per hour. It was only 20 minutes' flight time from Washington, D.C.

In no time, a makeshift memorial was erected to honor the 40 heroes of Flight 93. Nearly everyone who visited the site felt compelled to leave something of significance behind. It was as though you could share in their heroism by leaving a part of yourself at the site. I had been carrying a lucky coin since January of 1984. I had felt it and rubbed it so often that the image on the coin was almost rubbed away. It was a talisman of good tidings to me. On my one and only visit to the Flight 93 crash site, I left it on the flat surface of a two-by-four.

The crater that the plane created was immediately transformed into hallowed ground, since it was the burial site for those who willingly gave their lives so that others would live. Guards were hired 24/7 to protect the site against curiosity seekers, looters, and others who would defile it, intentionally or not.

One of those security guards was Robert Wagstaff,

hired on November 9, 2001. He and his fellow security guards were headquartered in a mobile home that was set up during the early investigation as a sort of command post.

In an interview with Linda Moulton Howe, Officer Wagstaff said he had experienced so many indications of haunting at that place that he had reservations about even entering the trailer alone.

One time as he and his partner were settling in for a night shift, there was a knock at the door. They went to the door but found nobody there. When they returned to the room they were using in the trailer, they found chairs newly set up for their card game. Shortly thereafter, they heard people walking through the trailer. They immediately heard people talking indistinctly outside the trailer. Again nobody was there. There weren't even footprints in the snow, which had recently fallen.

Another time, a spirit sat in Officer Wagstaff's personal vehicle and asked him, "So, now what?" Another spirit sat on the trunk of his car, compressing the springs under its weight. Then when Officer Wagstaff got out of the car and walked around to the rear, he saw the spring rebound when the spirit got off the trunk.

The most unsettling observation he made was when a young woman wearing jeans and a sweater walked toward him from the crash site. He was in his car at the main gate. She was 10 to 15 feet away from him. He was about to get out and ask her what she was doing at four in the morning in the snow, dressed as she was. As soon as he placed his hand on the door handle, she vanished. .

He often saw "shadow people" walking around the area, indistinct shapes that disappeared when he shone his spotlight on them.

A local newscaster, Renae Kluk, went to the crash site with Robert Wagstaff. While in the trailer she and he both heard footsteps on the metal stairs to the trailer's door. Of course, when they went to see, no one was there.

On September 10, 2011, one day short of ten years after this first shot was fired in the war against terrorism by these 43 regular, everyday Americans, the first phase of the Flight 93 National Memorial was dedicated.

The intensity of the heroic victims' emotions during their final seconds, as well as the abruptness of their horrific end, caused some of them to become spectral, perhaps permanently attached to the site.

***

Psychic Beverly LaGorga, while still developing her abilities paid a visit to this hallowed ground with her husband John and her son, Jeremy. Here is an excerpt from her soon to-be-released book, *"The Making Of A Psychic- We Don't Talk About Those Kind of Things,"* by Beverly LaGorga as told to Ed Kelemen:

"My family and I decided to visit the Flight 93 Memorial in Shanksville, Pennsylvania, where 40 heroic Americans lost their lives in the September 11 attacks. When they fought the hijackers to regain control of the plane, it crashed into the countryside at over 500 miles per hour and disintegrated.

We went there to pay our respects to these heroes. Traveling eastward on U.S. Route 30 was a pleasant ride, but as soon as we turned onto the road to the crash site, I felt the change. Tears oozed from my eyes and I had a heavy, foreboding feeling in my heart. We parked in the lot and walked to the dedication area. All my feelings intensified and I became more and more grief-stricken.

We looked out over the huge, empty, rolling field, where a solitary American flag ruffled in the breeze. Someone, maybe a park ranger, told us that the flag marked the exact spot where the plane had crashed into the ground. I could see that--and much, much more.

Pandemonium reigned. People were stumbling around, dazed. Some were crying and screaming for help. A man wearing a red tie and a blue dress shirt with its sleeves rolled to the elbow walked toward the nose of the airplane. He was cradling his left arm as though it was broken. A dazed-looking woman with brown curly hair held her bleeding right temple. Others milled about screaming for help. People were everywhere. The confusion and hysteria were so overwhelming that I started to shake and cry.

"Bev, Bev, what's the matter? Are you OK?" John was concerned.

"John, it's horrible. I've never seen anything like this. All these poor people, and there's nothing I can do for them."

He cradled me in those big powerful arms where I have always been able to feel safe and protected.

"Bev, do you want me to take you back to the car? Do you want to leave?"

Before I could answer, I saw a flight attendant waving her arms over her head to get attention and shouting out, "Hey! We're over here. Please! We need help!" I can't even remember whether I answered John because those feelings of utter helplessness and heartbreak had become unbearable.

I wished with all my heart that I could do something, anything to help.

"You *can* help. We're over here."

Oh, my God. The flight attendant had heard me!

I turned to John and told him that I was going to try to get these poor people to cross over, if I could. I knew that it was a massive undertaking, more difficult than anything I had ever tried to do before. And more important. If I could just get them to realize that they were dead and no longer belonged on this side, maybe they would cross over. I had no idea whether this would work.

I tried to explain to the flight attendant that the plane had crashed and nobody survived. I must have gotten through to her. She stopped what she was doing and stood there in shock.

"We're all dead?" she said. "I'm dead?" She turned to walk slowly away.

I was shaken out of my train of thought by my son tugging at me, complaining. It was too hot, he was hungry, and he wanted to leave now. I had had about all I could handle and wanted to leave as well. I've never been back.

I told John that I would like to see the site both before and after the memorial was built, but I'm not sure whether I can ever go back. Maybe some day."

***

Eight miles farther along brings us to Bald Knob Summit of the Allegheny Mountains, 2,906 feet above sea level. Another one and three quarter miles and we arrive at the world-famous Ship Hotel.

Pennsylvania's Haunted Route 30
The S. S. Grandview
Juniata

Then

Driving eastward on Route 30, we will crest Allegheny Mountain and start down the eastern flank. We can literally look down on some of the clouds scudding along through what looks like an infinite view of the rolling Pennsylvania countryside. The road curves to the right as it descends. We carefully negotiate the mountainous two-lane around that bend, painfully aware of the 1,000-foot drop to our right. Then it curves to the left.

Suddenly, at the apex of that curve, there it is-a full size twin-stack oceangoing passenger steamer precariously perched on the edge of the dropoff. A dozen or more cars are parked along the landward side of the ship, which happens to also be its port side. Then we see the huge letters on its keel announcing that it is the Grandview Point Hotel. Another sign proclaims that we can see three states and seven counties from its decks, which have strategically placed coin-operated binoculars. Inside a full-service restaurant bustles with smiling waitresses, and the aroma of freshly cooked food surrounds us. There are a number of rooms for guests to relax and shake off the road weariness before continuing their journey.

We have arrived at the most famous attraction along the country's first coast-to-coast highway, affectionately known as the Ship Hotel.

Unfortunately, for us to enjoy all the amenities of this unique place, we need to have been here before it fell into abject disrepair in the late 1980s. To even see it as a dilapidated, abandoned hulk we'd have to arrive before October 26, 2001, the night it burned to the waterline and became a memory.

People still stop here, at what has been renamed Mount Ararat Lookout, and gaze wistfully at the rubble of what was once a proud sentinel looking over hundreds of square miles. When two or more travelers come together, they share tales of the great Ship Hotel.

As we stand here on a moonlit, quiet night, there isn't even a breeze. But that doesn't stop the ghosts of past travelers from enjoying their visit. We hear the rattling of silverware, the tinkling of glassware, and muted conversation from the shades of former customers enjoying their supper. If we listen closely, we may hear the voice of a youngster marveling at the binoculars. "Look Dad, we can see forever from here!"

Forever? Probably not, but we have a window into the past opened for us to visit a long-lost treasure.

… And now.

***

Being careful on the long downhill slope, let's head east again. After about nine miles, keep a lookout for a dilapidated old wooden building on our left. We have arrived at one of Bedford County's most infamous places.

Ed Kelemen

Bedford's Best Bordello

Mann's Choice

Patty Wilson, in her compendium of Pennsylvania hauntings, *The Pennsylvania Ghost Guide, Vol. 1*, leads off with "The Best Little Whorehouse in Pennsylvania." She couldn't pass on the title, and I can't pass on alliteration, so I'm calling the place "Bedford's Best Bordello." I just like the sound of it.

Once upon a time, the historic Hotel Lincoln overlooked the countryside from the top of Tull's Hill Road in Mann's Choice, PA. Tull's Hill was named after the Tull family, 12 members of which were massacred during an Indian raid in 1777.

More than 200 years later, in 1988, an unwary Steve Hall and his wife Darlene purchased the property sight unseen at a sheriff's sale. From the outside it's not all that prepossessing a place, just a relatively square frame building of two and a half stories with a gabled roof and a center chimney. The inside was a different story. The walls and ceiling of the main barroom were riddled with bullets. Personal belongings were scattered from the second floor to the first in what appeared to be a rush by the previous occupant to escape.

One of the first things the Halls encountered as they started the refurbishment that would result in their opening an antique store in the former hotel was a blood-soaked patio table and chair. Two broken pool cues lay in the still-sticky blood. Nearby a bloody set of brass knuckles lay in mute testimony to the violence. Nobody could be found in the vicinity leaking copious amounts of the life-sustaining fluid. A police investigation revealed nothing.

However, during that investigation, the Halls learned that the former owner of the establishment was an extremely violent, unpredictable person by the name of Patrick Malley who had bought the building after being paroled from prison. He had served time for murdering his neighbor. Why? They had a disagreement.

Mr. Malley greeted customers by brandishing one of his many guns. When he grew irritated with someone, he blasted holes in the walls and ceiling to vent his anger.

Malley, his ex-hooker girlfriend, Donna Corrick, and her son, Robert Corrick, disappeared one day. Patrick eventually resurfaced in his hometown of Elkland. Living next door to him was a dangerous business; he shot and killed another next-door neighbor in Elkland and was sent to prison again. This time he wasn't paroled. His wonderful personality got him murdered in prison.

Don't think unkindly of Patrick. Okay, so he murdered a couple of people; he wasn't the best host along the highway. He was a perennial thorn in the side of the liquor law enforcement authorities, having broken every law on the books and a few that weren't. He wasn't the most neighborly of people. He defaulted on his loan at the bank. He grew a little pot in the backyard. He was given to violent outbursts. But he *was* charitable to a fault. Steve Hall came across a stack of unmailed envelopes. He had started to burn them when he found a small amount of money in one. Each of those envelopes, dozens and dozens of them, contained a few dollars. Furthermore, each was addressed to a charity. Patrick was, after all, at heart a philanthropist. Who'd a thunk?

Steve and Darlene noticed that their female customers had difficulty going up the stairs to view the antiques on the second floor. Some couldn't ascend the steps at all out of pure fright. Others got to the top only to experience cold air blowing on them from rooms 1 and 3.

Steve pieced the story together from local folk, but one day the cook from 1935 stopped by and verified it. A murder had taken place on the second floor.

Back in those days the second floor and the attic housed a brothel. The ladies of the attic were the lower-class whores, who had only a curtained-off cubicle in which to conduct their business. A customer would go to the attic, pay the entry fee, and pick from the girls who had their curtains opened. The second-floor ladies were a cut above. Each had her own room, small though it was. Men paid extra for the privacy and not having to climb to the attic.

One day the husband of one of the second-floor prostitutes stopped in to see her. When he found out that she was entertaining a lover instead of a client, he went berserk. Sex for money was okay; that was business.

Having sex for free, however, just wasn't right.

He roared all the way up the stairs and was only slightly slowed down by the locked door to Room 3. He smashed it open with one mighty kick of his foot and confronted the lovers. The fellow getting a free one was shot dead where he lay. The wife screeched and ran through the connecting door to Room 1 in a futile escape attempt. The husband caught up with her, stabbed her several times, and hung her body from the closet door in Room 1.

The husband was apprehended and tried for murder in Bedford. He was acquitted. The jury considered him the aggrieved victim of the crime of adultery.

The cook from 1935? When he stopped by to tell his story, he had to have been at least eighty years old, but he looked no more than forty.

Anyhow, the poor lady of the evening who came to her unfortunate end on the second floor has yet to leave. Steve has encountered her on at least three occasions. Twice, while locking up the antique store as was his punctual habit at 5:30 p m., he found her watching him in the floor-length mirror on the door at the end of the hallway.

He describes her as a woman in her thirties, a dirty blonde with long curling hair and a ruffled nightgown. When he tried to get a better look at her, she disappeared.

The last time he saw her was when he was awakened from a sound sleep before sunrise. He sensed that something was wrong at the antique store five miles away. Steve did a complete walkthrough of the store, checking everything, just as he did at closing time each night. He found nothing amiss. When he went down the hallway, something told him to look ahead. There she stood.

The Halls' little gray tiger cat likes to sleep in the doorway of Room 3. She lies there purring as though being seriously stroked. It appears that the blonde lady likes cats and vice versa.

A bit of research at the registrar of deeds office showed Steve that the property had often changed hands. In one eight-year stretch, it had eight different owners. Some owned it for only a few months. Steve asked some of the previous owners why they left. Their reasons ranged from bad health that miraculously cleared up when they sold to horrendous utility bills that bankrupted them. One owner said that each night he personally turned off all the appliances, lights, and power. In the morning, all the lights would be on, the french fryers would be bubbling, the stoves were on, and even the jukebox would be playing at full blast. The electric bill alone cost him hundreds of dollars a month. Someone didn't want him there.

Every one of the owners had tried to operate the place as a bar, but even though it was on a major highway just outside of Bedford, nobody could make a profit. Steve and Darlene believe the blonde woman caused the businesses to fail. When they sold the last piece of bar equipment, she was content. Nobody has seen her since--except the cat, and he's not about to snitch on someone who strokes him.

It is only reasonable that a haunted house would have haunted furniture. The Halls have an antique jelly cupboard that they are sure holds a haunt. In the 1800s there was no regulation of petroleum products. Kerosene could vary in quality from a barely burnable sludge to a mixture approaching gasoline in its volatility.

Pennsylvania's Haunted Route 30

Every day before dark it was the responsibility of one of the older children, usually the oldest girl, to trim, clean, fill, and light the kerosene lamps. The jelly cupboard provided a wide, stable base for the operation. Because the quality of the product varied so much, horrendous accidents could happen.

A ring is burned into the top of the jelly cupboard from the base of a kerosene lamp. A scorched area trails from there where the kerosene splashed, ran, and burned. The fire was so intense that one of the cupboard doors had to be replaced.

This cupboard makes noises every evening. It sounds like two tree limbs being rubbed vigorously together, followed by a banging or thumping that sounds like books falling over. As often as these sounds have been heard, nothing has ever been out of place in the room when people rush to investigate. It even happened one time while a TV crew was on the premises to do a feature on the hauntings.

The cat often runs up to the cupboard as if investigating it. When one of the Halls opens the door, she runs away. They believe that a girl burned to death when a kerosene lamp exploded in her face and she now haunts the last thing she saw while alive.

Behind the house sit two old, derelict ore locomotives. The property was once used by the Jamestown Quarry, Solvie Process Chemical Company from New York, which mined limestone to make concrete during World War II. The locomotive was used to gently back one coal car at a time up a rickety, dead-end trestle to the chute that would fill it with the crushed limestone.

One evening in the summer of 1947, the engineer of

Engine #49 fell asleep at the throttle. He leaned the wrong way against the throttle, nudged it open, and sent the train crashing off the dead end of the trestle one hundred feet down into the crusher building. The engineer never awakened during his final trip to oblivion at precisely 8 p.m.

It took nearly two years to repair and refit Engine #49 and get it back into service hauling crushed limestone from the quarry. Once again, on a warm summer evening at exactly 8 p.m., tragedy struck. A piece of equipment struck Engine #49 in such a way as to cause a high pressure steam line to burst. The new engineer was cooked alive by the superheated steam.

Understandably, after the second engineer's death, no one would work on or around Engine #49. The workers complained that when its boiler was fired, the smell of burning flesh permeated the area. No amount of cleaning the engine could fix the problem, so it was retired. It now sits in the back of the property, a rusted, stripped hulk with neither bell nor whistle. However, neighbors report that on certain warm summer nights at precisely 8 p.m., the sounds of a phantom train's bell and whistle are carried on the air as it plies its assigned route to no one knows where.

No wonder then that this property is haunted. At least fourteen deaths are known to have taken place here. Six people died in the building and eight more on the highway in front of it. At least the Halls have done what they could to send a number of them to a more restful place.

Let's head east Route 30 again. In less than a mile we will come to the intersection of Route 30 and PA Route 31.

The Jean Bonnet Tavern
Bedford

The Jean Bonnet Tavern, located at the juncture of US Route 30 and PA Route 31 a short distance west of US Route 220, has a long and rich history. Its earliest incarnation was as an unnamed French fort in the early 1700s.

In 1758, General John Forbes had occasion to stay at "the old abandoned French fort west of Bedford." While there, he apprehended and hanged a teamster who was observing troop movements with the intention of selling that information to the enemy. Wanting to neither upset nor inform the men outside the ruined fort, the General had the body buried within the ruins. Local historians knew better than to believe rumors, so they scoffed at this story for two centuries. Then in 1958, when new owners decided to refurbish the place, the basement was dug up. Skeletal remains of an individual with a broken neck were found. Bits of button and metal found with those remains dated to the mid-1700s. . This macabre story illustrates the powerful psychic energy that is present at this place.

Patty A. Wilson, author of *Pennsylvania Ghost Guide, Vol II,* has graciously granted permission to quote from a section titled "Return to the Haunted Jean Bonnet Tavern."

"Perhaps one of the most dramatic sightings occurred to a female bartender and her male friend years before Shannon and Melissa Jacobs, the present owners, had purchased the building. One night, the bartender was working when a friend of hers came in. Through the course of the evening, the fellow had too much to drink. When it came time to close up, she and her male companion were afraid to let the inebriated fellow drive. As the guy lived nearby, they decided to lock up, take the man home, and then return to finish cleaning up. The woman had the keys and knew this would be fine with the owners. They took the man home and returned to the bar. As they walked along the porch, they glanced in the window of the bar. Sitting there was a solitary man who was sipping a drink. That was impossible for they had made sure the bar was empty before leaving. Still, the fellow had gotten in somehow. Quickly, they unlocked the door and hurried into the bar. No one was there, but the building is big, so did the man hear them coming and hide? The two immediately ruled out anyone hiding in the upper levels because they had the key that unlocked the iron grillwork that separated the bar from those floors. However, someone could have gone down the stairs to the restaurant. They mounted a search but found no one. This upset the woman so much that after duly reporting the events to the owners; she did not often mention the story.

But employees are not the only ones to experience the hauntings. Guests reported many encounters as well. Scott Crownover decided to spend the night at the tavern to see if he would experience an encounter. He invited a group of friends and a few members of the Central Pennsylvania Paranormal Association along. The group would not be disappointed. They rented the attic apartment that was then for let and went down to the Tavern. Afterward, they went up to the bar, where one of the men felt someone touch him. While they were discussing that, a woman heard them and came over. She said that the conversation had caught her ear as she had just experienced being touched by someone at the edge of the bar a little earlier. She too insisted that no one was near her. Later that same evening, another member of the group, Al Brindza, was in the bar watching the activity. Now, Al is a confirmed nondrinker, so he felt a bit out of place in the bar. However, he tried to concentrate upon his feelings, despite the loud voices and the piano playing at the other end of the room. Suddenly he glanced at the one doorway that led into the hallway. Looking through the door were a group of people in rough clothes. Al called them "frontier type" clothes. The group was watching the man playing the piano at the other end. Al described his experience as "like trying to watch two televisions at once." He was aware of the real people at the bar, but he was equally drawn by those looking in from another time. This lasted a few seconds, but when he looked away and back again, they were gone."

Of course, new owner Melissa Jacobs has had her own experiences in the building. Soon after purchasing it, she began to notice that every time she went past the door to the then unrented attic apartment the door would be in a different position. If it was closed when she first passed it, then it would be wide open a few minutes later when she came by again. One morning she noticed this occurring several times and she decided that someone had gotten into the building somehow and was playing a trick on her. Melissa went to her office on the tavern second level to await a salesman who was coming in. When the man arrived, Melissa explained the situation to him and asked if he would accompany her on a search of the building. He agreed. The two went past the apartment, which was open as they began searching the bedroom level. A few moments later, they went by again, but it was closed. No one was found in the apartment or on any other level in the building, and the doors were all locked securely from the inside. The salesman was as baffled by the strange door as Melissa was."

The Jean Bonnet Tavern has been lovingly restored by its current owners, Shannon and Melissa Jacobs. It is much more than a haunted tavern. It is a warm and cheerful place to stay, with four comfortable rooms that are reasonably priced in a historic building with a great restaurant. If you spend the night in hopes of meeting one of the otherworldly denizens, and you just come away with just the satisfaction of a great night's sleep and warm hospitality, you will still be happy.

Stop in and wash the road dust from your throat. If you get the feeling that an unseen someone is staring at you, it's probably because someone is.

* * *

A short jaunt along Route 30 to Business Route 220 will bring us to the Old Bedford Village Archeological Site. Stop in and, if you're lucky, it'll be one of the days that they are serving their wonderful home-made soup.

Ed Kelemen

The Quaker School House

Old Bedford Village

220 Sawblade Rd.
Bedford

Old Bedford Village is an historical site which has live demonstrations of frontier living in beautifully restored and relocated buildings of bygone days. It has everything that a town of the 18th and 19th centuries needed: a tavern, a press, two schools, a theater, a church, a bakery, a candle shop, a general store, and even a jail. Check out the village's website for an up-to-date listing of activities ranging from Civil War reenactments to interactive Murder Mystery events.

The building that concerns us at the moment is the eight-sided Quaker School House built in Saint Clair Township elsewhere in the Bedford County in 1851 where it held classes until 1932. There are two stories that explain why the building was built in the shape of an octagon. The first is that, by having an opening such as a window or door on each of the eight sides, it allowed the building to use available daylight more efficiently, allowing a more even distribution of heat and ventilation. As an added bonus, it allowed the teacher to stand in a place of prominence giving all students an equal view. The second explanation is that it kept the devil out. Somehow, I prefer the first explanation.

Patty Wilson is a renown paranormal investigator, psychic, and author of over 20 books on the subject. What some people don't know is that she also appears at the village as a docent and teacher about the French and Indian War. Having had many experiences within the village, she made arrangements for the Ghost Research Foundation, of which she is a co-founder to conduct an investigation there. The results included EVP's of the regular activities that occur in a school: children giggling, chairs being scraped across the floor, and footsteps, a myriad of footsteps.

One of the things that prompted that investigation was an experience she had while a reenactment was underway. At the time Patty was portraying a schoolmarm at the school when a frightened little boy of about 7 ran into the building. He said that there were scary looking men outside with their faces all painted red and black. Patty, being aware of the reenactment going on, realized that it had to be one of the reenactors portraying an Indian. She collared one and asked him to come into the building to explain to the little boy that he was just an actor and wouldn't think of hurting anyone for real.

The fellow portraying an Indian got half-way to the school house and stopped in his tracks.

"Maybe you better bring the boy out for me to talk to him," he said.

Well she did and the little boy talked with him, even touching his feathers and face paint. Convinced of the harmlessness of the Indian reenactors, the little guy went back out to roam the village with his family.

When Patty expressed puzzlement about the reenactor's inability to enter the school house, he explained why.

"I want to apologize for not coming in, but I couldn't. When you were standing in the doorway there, there was a man standing behind you. He wasn't alive. He was a white man from the colonial period. He was very angry, upset that an Indian was coming into the school."

Just goes to show that spirits can manifest themselves under just about any conditions, even on a bright sunlit day, if their emotions are jarred enough.

**

Ok, back onto Route 30 and east to the town of Everett.

The Face in the Window

Everett

Time was there wasn't a cookie-cutter, brand-name, antiseptic, combination hotel-motel-eatery every place one road met another. Inns for weary travelers were few and far between. Overlooking the small town of Everett is a large old stone house that once served as a restful overnight stop for those who had last seen a roof over their heads at a tavern in Juniata Crossings some miles to the east. Many early settlers, traders, travelers, tinkers, and peddlers overnighted here.

Back in the 1700s, you didn't go to the store; the store came to you. Usually on the back of a peddler. Wealthy peddlers carried their stores in a wagon. Since there were very few wealthy peddlers, most carried a heavy box filled with what frontier families needed most: needles, patent medicines, tools, cooking utensils, and writing paper. Maybe a few plugs of tobacco.

These peddlers were always a welcome sight, and not just for the wares they carried. They were the news reporters of their day and were full of stories of all the towns along their route.

One of these peddlers used to stay at this inn above Everett to shake off the road grime, eat a good meal, and enjoy a comfortable night's sleep. Coming from the east one evening, he had a restful night. Then he took up his load and headed westward in the morning. The innkeeper and his family looked forward to seeing the peddler again on his return, when he would bring new products and news of the western towns along the path.

A few days later, the room where he had stayed was let to another traveler. At breakfast, the innkeeper's wife asked how he had spent the night.

"Quite well, dear lady," he replied, "except for the fellow who peeked in on me through the window of my room. You should tell your husband about him. I'll bet he's up to no good."

This puzzled the family, since they knew of no one who would do such a thing. Nevertheless, the parents instructed their children to keep a watchful eye. What with Indian raids, wild animals, and highwaymen about, you couldn't be too careful.

One night the daughter was making up the bed in that room when she screamed. She had seen a face peering in at her through the window. Everyone rushed to her assistance. She told them it was the peddler who had left the room more than a week ago. Why he would do such a thing, nobody could figure out. And nobody could find a trace of him around the property or outside the window.

A few days later, a traveler from Bedford arrived to spend the night. Of course the family asked for all the news. He said, "I suppose the most important news is of the finding of a dead peddler in the brush by the road not far from here. But I guess you already know about it."

"Certainly not," the innkeeper responded. "Can you describe him?"

By the time the traveler had finished his story, the family knew the identity of the poor victim left along the road. It was the peddler who had stayed with them.

"How long ago was this?" the wife asked.

"More than a week now, ma'am. I'm sure that whoever killed him is gone by now."

The family looked at one another. The peddler had been killed a full two days *before* he had appeared at the window.

Over the next few weeks, other customers complained of the fellow who looked in on them through the window of the bedroom. Something had to be done, or business would be lost. With typical frontier logic, the innkeeper solved the problem. He simply walled up that window. No more complaints were received.

III

The Center of the State

Pond Bank
South of Fayetteville

At the beginning of the twentieth century, life was difficult for almost everyone. There was no medical insurance, even if you had the money to pay for it. If you lost your job, you could starve to death. Unemployment insurance didn't exist. Only the very lucky graduated from high school. Most people had to go to work while still in grade school to survive.

In some ways, it was worse in the countryside, where everything depended on the success or failure of this year's crop. In other ways, it was better in the country, where everybody knew everybody and everyone pulled together and shared when necessary.

Except for the single mother. A widow with a dowry was one thing. A young woman with a child was something else entirely. No woman wanted another invading her home and hearth. No man wanted the instant expense of raising someone else's child. An unmarried mother was also disdained because she was said to be of "loose morals."

No future. A sordid past. Unwanted. Friendless.

Destitute. And a baby on her hip. It's a small wonder that the poor girl was driven to despair. One evening she and her baby went for a walk by the pond that gives this place its name. When she came to the shoreline, she didn't stop. She continued into the cold water until it covered both of them, ending their young lives. At some point she lost track of her baby in the depth of the murky water of that pond. She is still searching for that child to this day.

Due to her ethereal appearance, she is known as the White Lady when she hitches rides in cars and trucks. Imagine having her suddenly appear in the bed of your pickup truck or trail behind your taillights in the evening mists.

Or worse, having her appear suddenly in the beams of your headlights on one of these dark and twisting rural roads. There are two known instances of that happening. In one, the driver lost control, swerving from side to side until his car came to an abrupt stop when meeting a less than compliant tree. A little while later, the police arrived to take an accident report and arrange for the vehicle to be towed to a repair facility. The bewildered driver attempted to explain to the officers how the sudden appearance of a lady in a gauzy white gown caused him to wreck his car.

The two first officers at the scene nodded knowingly at his story and went back to their cruiser to radio headquarters to warm up the Breathalyzer. The third officer intervened, telling them that there was no need for it.

He was the person who experienced the other occurrence.

Ed Kelemen

The Cashtown Inn

1325 Old Route 30

Cashtown

Care for another meal in a fine historic establishment? Our next stop is the Cashtown Inn, sometimes called the most haunted building in the Gettysburg area. It has its own book, called, appropriately enough, *Haunts of the Cashtown Inn,* by Suzanne and Bob Wasel Gruber. It's been featured on episodes of the popular television series *Ghost Hunters,* on the Syfy channel. Before that, it was on the long-running *Mysterious Journeys.*

What has made this medium-size B&B with an

acclaimed restaurant so popular with those who investigate the paranormal? Simple: a few days at the end of June and the beginning of July, 1863. You see, a little thing called the Battle of Gettysburg happened along Route 30 about eight miles east of here. Some say the battle had its start within these brick walls.

The inn came to be out of necessity. As frontiersmen found gaps and pathways through the mountains, traffic between eastern and western Pennsylvania increased dramatically. Settlers headed west to start new lives and traders traveled in both directions to serve and supply them. One such place was built here at the foothills of the mountains in 1797. The innkeeper was responsible for travelers' overnight accommodations as well as for collecting tolls from those who wished to travel the road. Early on he learned of the impecunious nature of his clientele and stopped extending credit. The inn's reputation for demanding cash up front grew. It became known as the Cashtown Inn and shared its name with the hamlet that grew up around it.

It was a peaceful, sleepy place for its first six decades, just a comfortable stop on the way east or west. Then, in late 1862, it was discovered by Major General James Ewell Brown ("Jeb") Stewart of the Confederate Army on one of his famous foraging circumnavigations of the Union Army. He was the first of many Confederate generals to partake of the Cashtown Inn's hospitality.

A scant half-year later, the inn became the headquarters for the Confederate Army of Northern Virginia when General Ambrose Powell Hill took up residence there on June 29, 1863. By this time the Confederate Army was far from home, and its supply line was stretched to the utmost. When General Henry Heth asked if General Hill had any objections to his men entering Gettysburg to find shoes and other supplies, General Hill is said to have remarked, "None at all." And events were set in motion that could not be stopped.

During the next few days, the inn would become a hospital for wounded soldiers. So many amputations and surgeries were carried out on the premises that the little stream nearby ran red with their blood. The stack of amputated limbs thrown out the basement window grew so high that the sunlight couldn't penetrate it; further operations were performed by lamp and candle light.

During the battle, the inn remained General Hill's headquarters as the entire Army of Northern Virginia passed it en route to Gettysburg, then passed it again in defeat on its way back to Virginia. In its wake, it strewed death, destruction, and the spirits of those who were so emotionally tied to the place that even death couldn't release them.

Stand across the road from the Cashtown Inn. Who is that on the second floor looking out the second window from the left ? Was he the lookout watching for the pursuing Yankees at the end of the battle? Or was he just marveling at the heavy traffic that suddenly appeared in this sleepy town some 150 years ago?

In 1905 a photographer took a picture of the front of the inn. When he developed the film, a young man in a Confederate uniform was standing on the front porch. That soldier wasn't there when the picture was snapped.

Another time, renovations were going on in the inn. The owners were sleeping in a room on the second floor when the wife was awakened by the sounds of heavy items being moved about in the attic. Fearing ridicule, she didn't awaken her husband. But the noise woke him anyway. She asked if he was going to go up and check on the noise. He replied, "Maybe in the morning."

People staying in Room 4 often wake up in the middle of the night to the sound of someone knocking on their door. Answering the door is an exercise in futility because there is never anybody there.

A writer staying in Room 4 was roused from bed by the sound of three sharp raps on the door three separate times one night. He wondered what message the entity at the door was trying to convey, but he never found out.

A former owner was constantly asked about the person in a Confederate uniform in Room 4, the adjacent hallway, or the doorway leading into the bar. A stuffed teddy bear in Room 4 has a mind of its own. A paranormal investigator staying there placed it just so before retiring. In the morning, it was turned 90 degrees so that it could see out the window.

In Room 3, the A. P. Hill room, a ghostly figure has been making an appearance at the window for the last 30 years.

Room 5 has had activity of such intensity that guests have abandoned it during the night. A ghostly apparition strolls through the room, followed by the sound of heavy breathing from the empty rocking chair.

One fellow staying overnight was forcibly yanked from his bed by something unseen. He was so shaken that he left his room and spent the night on the front porch.

One group of guests asked the innkeeper about the cold spots in the room and the inconsiderate man whose horse had awakened them during the night by snorting and clomping beneath their window. When they returned from informing the staff about this inconvenience, they found their luggage all packed and ready to go.

The current owner, Jack Paladino, says guests have reported mysterious sounds, cigar smoke, boot steps, cries of children, and apparitions. He himself was once pushed from behind by an unseen entity.

***

A short trip eastward brings us to the most haunted place in America, the Gettysburg battlefield. But first we will come to yet another tavern that has refused to loose the ties that bind certain spirits within its halls.

The Herr Tavern and Publick House

900 Chambersburg Road

Gettysburg

Almost within sight of the Gettysburg Battlefield lies the Herr Tavern and Publick House. Originally called the Sweeney Stand, it was built in 1815 on the old stage road, now called Chambersburg Pike, Route 30, or the Lincoln Highway. Whatever you call the road, it leads right into the heart of the town that became famous for bloodshed. Mr. Sweeney wasn't overly endowed with business acumen; he went bankrupt in 1827. Frederick Herr purchased the property, renamed it the Herr Tavern and Publick House, and made a go of it. Perhaps part of Mr. Herr's success came from his home-brewed whiskey.

    Local lore has it that he supplemented the income from the tavern with money from a counterfeit operation in the basement and a brothel upstairs. In any case, it was a quiet place to lift a mug, sip a whiskey, and enjoy a good lunch or dinner. For three dozen years, that's just what it was: a quiet place.

    On June 26, 1863, the quiet was interrupted by a contingent of Confederate soldiers on their way to Gettysburg, foraging for supplies. The long march from Virginia had exhausted their supplies, emptied their stomachs, and worn out their shoes. They commandeered whatever they wanted. But they weren't thieves. They paid for what they took—but with worthless Confederate script. Warned of their approach, many Gettysburg merchants attempted to flee east across the Susquehanna River with everything they could tote, drag, or trundle.

For a couple of days, things quieted somewhat. Then on June 30, Union cavalry headed west on the Chambersburg Pike, whose fourth name was the Cashtown Pike. They made their headquarters at the Herr Tavern and set out pickets. The next morning they were confronted with a huge cloud of dust raised by the troops of Confederate General Heth heading right at them. Lieutenant Marcellus Jones of the United States 8th Illinois Volunteer Cavalry borrowed a Sharps carbine from Private George Heim, took aim at "a Confederate officer on a white or light gray horse," and fired. This started the most famous, one of the bloodiest, and arguably the most important battle of the Civil War. Over the next three days more than 150,000 American soldiers would battle one another to determine the fate of the Union. Nearly one of every three would become a casualty.

The inn changed hands that first day of the battle and became a field hospital. During this war, the primary purpose of field hospitals was the amputation of limbs. Soldiers who received head, chest, or stomach wounds were set aside to die; nothing could be done for them. But soldiers with shattered limbs might be saved if the damaged limbs were removed. That is, if infection from the unsanitary ten-minute operation didn't kill them. During battles, painkilling medications were notoriously scarce, especially for the Confederate Army.

The inn became hell on earth. Screaming wounded and dying men were left lying in rows awaiting the surgeons' skills while the battle raged on around them. A cannon shell crashed through the second-floor corner of the inn while operations were being carried out in every available space. Amputated arms, legs, hands, and feet piled up on the ground outside every window of the building.

So much blood was spilled that it fouled the drinking water from the well. Days after the battle, when the silence of death had descended on the little farming town, men were still being sickened from the water at the inn's well. It was decided to pump out the well to allow the water to freshen. One of the workers, relating the incident in a letter, wrote, "By and by, here comes up a little piece of a wrist and thumb."

Frederick Herr kept running the tavern until his death in 1868. During the following century it saw use as a hotel, a school of music, and a private residence. In 1977 it was purchased by Steve Wolf, who restored it to "the tavern-stand and publick house," that once again offered a peaceful, quiet place for travelers to enjoy a respite from their journeys.

During this renovation, the hauntings became obvious. Perhaps the spirits didn't like being disturbed by all the goings-on. One of the workers encountered a distinctly unfriendly presence that tried to push her down a flight of stairs. She yelled, "I'm just trying to turn it into a tavern again!" The thought of future medicinal libations must have mollified the spirit. Ever after that encounter, she felt accepted within the walls.

Mr. Wolf relates an encounter that he and a friend had one night. The two of them were alone in the tavern at opposite ends of the bar. They both distinctly heard someone at the bar between them ask for a beer. After ascertaining that it was neither of them who wished to slake their thirst, they concluded that it was the spirit of a long-dead customer or even Frederick Herr himself. They shared this encounter with a friend of theirs later. When that friend scoffed, an invisible hand gripped his shoulder and forced him from his barstool. He stopped laughing.

A spirit named Jack, who communicated through a ouija board, indicated buried treasure in the basement. If true, it has yet to be unearthed.

After a while, the upstairs of the building was converted into a B&B, perhaps recalling its days as the Reynolds Hotel. Room 1 was the original location of the Herrs' bedroom. One night, a lady was dozing on the bed with her young son beside her when someone shook her shoulder roughly. Her son slept on and she spent the rest of the night with her arms crossed protectively over her chest. Maybe Frederick and his wife don't like to share their room.

Guests have remarked on all the noise caused by someone moving furniture in the attic during the night. Sometimes things are heard being forcibly moved in adjacent rooms, but invariably the room is deserted.

One of the duties of the staff is to ensure that all the lights in the tavern are extinguished when they leave for the night. From time to time, looking back at the building as they enter their cars, they see a light on, a light that they know they turned off. Nevertheless, someone has to go back into the tavern and turn the light off again.

There is the man who clomps about in heavy boots upstairs, but the morning manager can never seem to catch up with him. Closed doors open and open doors close on their own. Sometimes doors lock and unlock themselves. Phantom water has been heard running so often in the kitchen sink that nobody bothers to check on it any more. Trays of dishes are heard crashing to the floor and pots are noisily tossed into the sink, but nobody can be seen.

Sometimes the spirits must be starved for entertainment, because TV sets in rooms 1 and 4 turn on all by themselves. Maybe the spirits have heard guests complain about cold spots and that's why they turn heaters on during the summer.

One night a credit card machine started spewing forth paper for no known reason.

The employees frequently interact with the spirits of the inn and have found them to be nice (or at least not actively malignant) and polite.

Each room has a guest diary where those fortunate enough to stay here record their experiences, comments, and compliments. Reading these diaries shows even the casual reader that the spirits shaken by Civil War battles have not yet resumed their rest.

***

Less than a mile on down Route 30 brings us right into Gettysburg and the National Battlefield Park.

Ed Kelemen

Gettysburg National Battlefield Park

Gettysburg

R oute 30 runs right through Gettysburg, considered the most haunted place in all of the United States. I will not attempt to go into detail on all the Gettysburg hauntings. Entire books have been written about them. If you do decide to investigate the ghosts of Gettysburg, allow plenty of time. It cannot be done in a day. Likewise, the battlefield at Gettysburg cannot be absorbed in one day, or even one visit. If you visit Gettysburg, you will be back. Take my word for it.

That being said, A young multiple award-winning poet from Ligonier, PA has been able to capture the essence and atmosphere of the Gettysburg Battlefield.

She has graciously granted permission for it to be included here.

***

I proudly present
Gettysburg
by
Paisley Adams

As I walk, the damp air of ages manifest,
Fog obscures my path, its tendrils form
Arms; horses and legs materialize in the night.
I recall where I tread and know who they are.
Faint echoes of their urgent howling arouse me.
They seem top not take yield to the living's heart
But gallop in a charge of such velocity
The translucent mouths of the gaping stallions foam,
Coming in a grim procession.
At me they gallop, their bayonets fastened with haste.
I wince, praying that these slain souls do not slay me.
Alas, the horse on gliding mist does nay halt,
The brigade of he netherworld, undaunted,
Gaseous bodies and rambunctious hooves helter-skelter.
I feel all but a cold gust, uharmed by the men.
They pass through me like shadows.
Then one battered, ragged-coated general turns,
Grinning with a fatherly smile.
With a resolute gesture of salute, he then winks.
Again he rides into the luminescent sea of phantoms.
The forms fade and blend into a musty fog.
I stride away, my mind in a blur.
At home, I gaze upon a rusted blade, a faded photo.

Ed Kelemen

I smile, knowing that I'd seen him
At Gettysburg.

As you tour the battlefield, you will eventually come to the spot where Pickett's Charge brought the Confederate forces as far north as they ever got. This place, where a friend of mine had a harrowing experience, is known as the High Water Mark.

High Water Mark
Gettysburg National Battlefield Park

The fence at the High Water Mark

After three days of withering battle, General Robert E. Lee decided to risk all in a frontal assault on Union lines. Against the advice of General Longstreet, Lee ordered Generals Longstreet, Pettigrew, and Pickett to attack the center of the Union lines under the command of General George Meade. The attack across 1,000 yards of open ground, with cannon fire raking the ranks of the Confederates from the front and the sides, lasted 50 minutes and yielded 10,000 casualties. This attack came to be known as Pickett's Charge.

It is customary in cities, villages, and towns that have been flooded for someone to draw a line on a wall to show exactly how far the water has encroached. That line is the high-water mark. On one side of the copse of trees on Cemetery Ridge is a monument that depicts an open book, titled "High Water Mark of the Rebellion." It lists all the valiant units of both the North and the South who fought here that day to determine the fate of a nation. It is placed at the point of the most northern incursion into the United States by Confederate troops. Perhaps it should be called "The High Blood Mark," since the ground was soaked with blood.

A friend of mine, Keven P., has been a Civil War re-enactor for much of his life. A true son of America, he has ancestors who fought on both sides during that first week of July 150 years ago. His ancestor who fought for the Union is a rather distant one, while his great-great-grandfather fought for the Confederacy in the Army of Northern Virginia, so it is only natural that he took on the persona of a Confederate rifleman.

In his teens, Keven took part in a re-enactment on the actual battlefield of Gettysburg. He was to be among those who would recreate the ill-fated Pickett's Charge. His unit was assigned to charge the Union line at that high-water mark." Then, honor of honors for a young man, he was selected to be one of the handful of soldiers who actually broke through the Union lines near the copse of trees. Kev says that he was elated and determined to perform honorably.

Just as it happened on that day so long ago, Keven and many other young men marched shoulder to shoulder in woolen uniforms of gray and butternut brown. When a man fell, the line was tightened up to fill the hole. And the men continued, shoulder to shoulder.

After being nearly destroyed at the Emmittsburg Road, the Sons of the South, an entire generation of America's best, reformed their units and continued their march toward the ridge ahead. Their objective was easy to see; it was marked by a small clump of trees at the center of the Union line.

More men fell by the wayside, their bodies littering the ground. Noses burned with the smell of gunpowder, and ears rang from the din of war. Things got confusing. The fog of war had descended on the troops and they knew only one thing—continue forward. The troops they were attacking were also enveloped in that red haze known as the fog of war. All they knew was that they must hold their line no matter what, even if it cost them their very lives.

Keven came to the low wall of stones and branches used as a small measure of protection by the Union soldiers. It wasn't much, but it was more than he had. He clambered over the wall and fell.

One of his legs gave out on him. It just quit working. "Ed," he told me, "it was just like it wasn't even there. I couldn't move it or anything. Hell, I couldn't even feel it." His comrades broke through the Union lines, advancing as far as the copse of trees before being beaten back, but he wasn't with them.

Keven was carried from the field of battle just like hundreds of others on the fateful day a century and a half ago. He wasn't left to what mercy could be garnered from a primitive field hospital where the offending limb would be amputated and tossed onto a pile of other shattered body parts. Instead, he was examined by paramedics in a state-of- the-art advanced-care ambulance equipped with radio communication with the nearest emergency room. At the hospital, examination, x-rays, MRIs, nor other tests found anything wrong with Keven's leg. Medical personnel adopted a wait-and-see attitude. Over the next few days, both feeling and movement returned to his leg until it was 100% once again.

Some time later, Keven learned that his great-great-grandfather had his leg blown off by canister shot at the exact location where his own leg lost feeling.

Coincidence? You be the judge. It's just one of thousands of mysterious incidents on the hallowed battlefield of Gettysburg.

Stay for a while and soak up the atmosphere. Realize what great events took place on the very ground where you are walking. Stop in at 271 Baltimore Street in the heart of town and sign up for one of the original Ghosts of Gettysburg Candlelight Walking Tours, based on the books by historian Mark Nesbitt

The built-up area bisected by Route 30 is where a number of ghostly folk call home. Here are some choice ones.

Pennsylvania's Haunted Route 30

York College

441 Country Club Road

Spring Garden

Just about a mile south of the center of York lies York College on Country Club Road. Given the age and history of this institution of higher learning, the fact that it's haunted isn't unusual. What is strange is that it isn't more haunted. Just about the time our nation's constitution came into being, in 1787, a two-story brick school called York County Academy opened up for the purpose of training elementary school teachers. In 1929, the Academy merged with another small private college to become the York Collegiate Institute and moved into larger quarters in the city. That building was destroyed by fire and rebuilt. The institute survived the ravages of the Great Depression as well.

In 1941, the institute acquired 57-1/2 acres just

outside of the city and became York Junior College. Its ranks of students were swelled by returning World War II vets and again by Korean War vets. The acreage that it had acquired allowed its expansion and still serves as its campus to this day.

In 1968, another major expansion took place. New administration buildings, academic buildings, and dorms were erected, and the school became York College of Pennsylvania. No longer exclusively a teacher's college, York College offers more than 50 undergraduate degrees as well as masters' and doctoral programs.

Colleges are notorious places for hauntings and strange occurrences, some of which do not originate from frat party over-imbibing.

Campbell Hall is at the center of the campus in more ways than one. It is where all students come to get their parking passes, change majors, and seek guidance. It is also where the college haunts tend to hang out. They make their presence known by knocking on doors and windows and uttering strange guttural sounds just out of sight.

An aggressive presence has been reported in the kitchen by students and staff alike. No one knows what has caused the hauntings or where they have come from. Likewise, nobody knows what causes the entity in the kitchen to be unsociable. One suggestion is that a disgruntled cook feels that the food wasn't appreciated enough.

***

Back in the City of York is a structure that is a bit more malevolent, the old abandoned prison of York.

Pennsylvania's Haunted Route 30

The Old Abandoned Prison of York

Chestnut Street

York

In 1853, a brooding brick and stone edifice opened on Chestnut Street to house York County's malefactors. In 1905, it was expanded and enlarged without alleviating any of the conditions that made it such a cruel place. The cells were arranged in tiers with a large open area in the center. It had its very own place for executions, called the Hanging Hook.

The old place closed in 1979, replaced by a new corrections housing establishment that resembles a college campus--except for the floodlights and razor-wire-topped chain-link fence.

No prison is a place that most people would like to visit, but the old prison was hell. It was brutally hot in the summer and unbearably frigid in the winter. One prisoner reported that the only meat he had seen during his stay was rancid venison that a state trooper had recovered: road kill. For a time, white and black prisoners were segregated and even had different visitation days. When the prison needed to house a woman, she spent her sentence in the padded cell reserved for prisoners who should have been patients at the local mental hospital. Officials felt that it would be too much trouble to open a cell just for females.

This place was witness to much brutality, including murder and torture. It is unknown how many of the prisoners' who fell to their death from the tiers of cells did so accidentally. Many were found hanging in their cells. Others had their throats slashed with shivs.

One unfortunate soul managed to steal a horse to facilitate his escape. He didn't get far. He was apprehended on the steps of the Christ Lutheran Church, where punishment was administered by his pursuers. If you come across a raggedly dressed, shoeless fellow in nineteenth-century garb morosely roaming the area, it's probably him. He isn't dangerous.

Visitors to the dungeon-like premises have been escorted by a small group of ghostly occupants. When they get up the second and third-floor cellblocks, people see the glow of a lighted cigarette moving along the block, bobbing up and down as though dangling from someone's lips. But no one is ever found, and cigarette smoke is never smelled.

It isn't hard to understand how you could lose not only your freedom but your mind in this place.

Pennsylvania's Haunted Route 30

The Phantom Biker of York

Arsenal Road

York

Motorcycle riders are inordinately proud of their mounts. The give them names and frequently refer to them as, "She." For every hour astride their iron horse they spend at least an equal amount of time lavishing care on her. Seldom is a rider seen on a bike that has been polished to less than perfection, every square inch of chrome reflecting the sunlight, the fenders and tank are waxed to the point that they can be used for mirrors. The, "Bike," as riders call it, is tuned until it cannot be tuned any more. Each stray speck of dust is hunted down like vermin and carefully removed lest it detract from the overall perfection of the bike.

Harley riders are even more attached to their bikes, spending thousands and thousands of dollars over and above the purchase price to individualize them. And there is nothing to compare to the brand loyalty of the Harley rider. Most would rather walk than ride any other brand.

York, PA is the mecca for Harley riders and owners. For this is where the Harley Davidson Vehicle Operations Center is located. During operating hours tours of the facility can be taken and demo rides are offered. All Harley riders try to make the pilgrimage to York, PA at least once.

The Harley facility is located on Arsenal Road, a wide 4-lane, relatively straight boulevard with traffic signals every so often. It is reminiscent of Van Nuys Boulevard in California. And like that legendary strip of road, it is a popular place to wind up your bike and let go. But, that's only by those people from out of town. The local police also know what a popular place Arsenal Road is for bikers to let go and they keep a tight lid on it.

But, nevertheless, pride is pride. During those hours between closing time at the bars and sunrise when anything can and does happen, a solitary biker sits at one of the red lights waiting for it to change. Perhaps he is wondering why it isn't set to automatic like all the other lights in the world at this time of night. So, he sits there, revving the engine and thinking about just running the light that his bike isn't large enough to trigger.

Suddenly, a large chopper arrives beside him at the light. The empty eyes behind the old goggles stare across disdainfully at the biker, and the cadaverous face twists into a bit of a sneer when he takes the lit cigarette from his lips and offers it to the rider who arrived first at the light.

The challenge is unmistakeable. The question doesn't need to be spoken, "Wanna Drag?" And pride is pride. The light goes green. Both bikes roar from the light, holding their revs high, and accelerating through the gears until speeds are reached that the road was never intended to witness. But that damn chopper stays just a little ahead of the other bike, like it is teasing. The next red light is approaching at an insane speed and there is cross traffic.

Pride is pride, but sanity is also sanity and the rider backs off, downshifting and braking as the chopper roars through the intersection disappearing in a gray cloud of exhaust and tire smoke. That's when our lone rider hears the wail and whoop of the siren of one of York's finest.

When the rider tries to explain why he showed

disdain for the speed limit, telling the officers that it is in the wee hours of the morning, he wasn't hurting anyone, he stopped at the light, and he wasn't drinking. Could they please, just this once, given him a break? He is talking to deaf ears, they have heard it all before.

Maybe he gets indignant, just a little, at this point. He asks them about the other bike, the chopper. Why didn't they go after him? He was the instigator. Once again, he is talking to deaf ears. They have heard it all before. And there is never any other chopper.

***

Just about a mile south of Route 30, on PA Route 24, lies Camp Security. A historical marker on East Market Street in Springett Township directs you to it.

Ed Kelemen

Camp Security

York

There were only a handful of prisoner of war camps during the Revolutionary War. Camp Security is the last one that remains largely unmolested--but perhaps not for long. A developer is strenuously trying to develop the land for "upscale housing." Go to the Friends of Camp Security at www.campsecurity.com to see how this latter-day Revolutionary War battle is being fought.

In 1781, British General Burgoyne surrendered his troops at Saratoga, New York. Camp Security was built to house those soldiers and their families for the duration of the war. The population of the camp was increased by those captured at the Battle of Yorktown, Virginia, bringing the inmate population to 1,500. The camp wasn't much, just a stockade and a village of little wooden huts, but it served its purpose well until 1783, when the war ended and the prisoners were offered repatriation. When a large number of the prisoners decided to stay and throw in their lot with the hardy pioneer folk of the area, their decision spoke volumes about the treatment they had received during their enforced stay in Pennsylvania.

People walking the crisscrossed pathways of the ancient camp experience that well-known feeling that they are not alone. Sometimes they encounter the ghost of a British soldier. Perhaps he was left behind when the offer of repatriation was made.

Leaving the city of York, Old Route 30 follows PA State Route 462 for a ways. If you take a right turn onto Cool Creek Road before you get to Wrightsville, you will find Eastern York High School about two and a quarter miles along the road.

Ed Kelemen

Eastern York High School

Cool Creek Road

Lower Windsor

Eastern York School District serves the needs of about 2,800 students in five schools. Its high school is the home of the Golden Knights football team. It is also the home of several few disturbing entities.

The drama group at the school has put on some really ambitious musicals for such a small school. Recent ones include *Beauty and the Beast, Grease, Hello Dolly,* and *Les Miserables*. When a small group puts on an ambitious Broadway production, it takes a lot of time. Frequently that time extends way past school hours.

Students who have spent those extra hours rehearsing, building sets, and arranging scenery have had strange encounters. Someone or something paces agitatedly back and forth on the catwalk over the auditorium, footsteps echoing down to the thespians. No matter how many times the noise has been investigated, its origin has never been found. A stifling feeling of being trapped permeates the auditorium area to the point that sometimes students check the doors to make sure they aren't locked.

Students walking the deserted hallways have had an unsettling experience. This boy's story is typical: He was blithely strolling along, mind occupied with those thoughts that keep young people entertained, and listening to music on an MP3 player. Suddenly his pleasant reverie was interrupted by the sound of a locker door slamming shut.

"That's weird," he thought, because he was the only live person in the hallway, but he put it out of his mind. Then it got weirder. A nearer locker door slammed shut. The boy picked up the pace a bit. Another door, even nearer, slammed. Then another and another, nearer still slammed shut without human aid. The student started trotting, looking over his shoulder, but he saw no one. The faster he moved, the closer the slamming got. Then, just as it seemed that whoever was slamming the doors was about to overtake him, it stopped. Silence reigned again in the hallway, but peace had fled before the boy's fear.

Ed Kelemen

***

Let's brood over this for a while as we go back to Route 30 and head east once more. Maybe we are feeling a tad empty in the tummy. No problem. We can stoke up at our next stop while thinking about the haunts that may join us.

Pennsylvania's Haunted Route 30

The Accomac Inn

6330 River, Dr.

York

A mile north of Route 30 on River Road is the Accomac Inn, a place of fine dining, great service, and a fantastic view of the Susquehanna River. With nearly 300 years of history on the site where ferries, inns, and taverns have been located, it is no wonder that it has gathered its share of haunts.

Workers encounter strange happenings after hours while cleaning the dining rooms. Dishes move on their own. Doors open, then close by themselves. Even tables and chairs move about unaided. And all the while, ethereal music and a soft woman's voice are heard.

This haunting started in the late 1800s. You see, the building was originally the home of the Coyle family, consisting of Johnny Coyle and his father and mother. Johnny's father tilled the soil around the farmhouse and also worked as a ferryman on the river.

Mr. Coyle hired a young woman named Molly to help out around the farm. Johnny immediately fell deeply, helplessly, and hopelessly in love with her. (He was an easily impressed and probably quite horny young man.) Anyhow, he asked her to be his woman. It has not been reported whether this was a proposal of marriage or a crudely worded request for an assignation. It really makes no difference; she emphatically rebuffed his advances.

Poor Johnny just couldn't take this affront to his masculinity, so he killed her in a blind rage in the old barn near the farmhouse. The barn burned to the ground during the 1950s, and there is now a parking lot where that mute witness to murder once stood.

Johnny was arrested for the deed, tried, convicted, and hanged, all in a relatively short period of time. His guilt was obvious, so there was no bother about appeals and such things. After the hanging, his family buried him about 100 yards from the farmhouse. A stone marks his grave. The epitaph on it reads, "Weep not, Mother, for I am not dead, but merely sleeping." No mention is ever made about how the remains of his poor victim were treated.

About a year after the old barn burned to the ground, the farmhouse also burned. Unlike the barn, it was rebuilt and eventually turned into an upscale restaurant, which it is to this day. If you search about 100 yards to the north of the inn, you can still find Johnny's grave.

Johnny and Molly still inhabit the inn in spirit. Apparently she didn't hold a grudge against her murderer, at least not for long. They enjoy playing pranks, breaking dishes, and hiding things. An employee saw a pair of spirits in an upper-floor storage room. A man and a woman, she said, both in their twenties.

Johnny has achieved in death what was denied him in life--the companionship of the object of his obsession. Much the same as the relationship that Claude Benedum was able to reignite with the love of his life after he perished of pneumonia in Flanders Fields. Remember his circumstances at Chatham College in Pittsburgh?

***

Let's keep heading east on Route 30 and find some more happy and not-so happy haunts.

IV

Approaching the City of Brotherly Love

Lancaster County Prison

625 East King Street

Lancaster

Main Entrance to the Castle of Confinement

East King Street in Lancaster follows the path of Old Route 30 before the bypass was built. Eventually it merges back onto present-day Route 30.

As we drive along, we will come to what looks like a Norman castle and keep on our left. Its turreted facade and battlements look out of place on this quiet, tree-lined street. It is no stretch of the imagination to daydream about dungeons, tortures, and life sentences carried out within its cold stone walls.

Humane treatment of criminals wasn't part of the vernacular in the early days of our nation. There was no actual "prison system." Each prison operated independently and pretty much made up the rules as it went along.

Felons sentenced to life in prison inside the Castle must have been viewed as extreme escape risks. Not only were they confined to cells, but they were chained to the walls of those cells. To further inhibit their mobility, concrete blocks were chained to their feet. Prisoners sentenced to death were held in those cells, in those chains, until it was time to go to the scaffold. The tradition of a sumptuous final meal hadn't yet begun, so with empty stomachs, they were led through a crowd of jeering citizens for whom public hangings were the only dramatic entertainment they could afford.

Those old cells and chains are still there, and this inhumanity to our fellow man in the name of justice gives chills to visitors. Look at that brownish mark on the floor of the cell. Is it a rust mark—or dried blood?

Listen intently. Maybe you will be one of the ones who hear tuneless whistling wafting on the air. Or is that the breathy rustle of dry whispering as long-gone prisoners try desperately to communicate with one another?

Franklin and Marshall College

628 College Avenue

Lancaster

Just goes to show, if you want your name on a building, bridge, or institution, send money. It works today and it worked in our country's formative years. In 1787, Benjamin Franklin's generous contribution allowed the construction of one of the first institutions of higher learning in the United States. No wonder then, that it was called Franklin College. Its very first class included 78 men and 36 women, making it the first coeducational institution in the country. The first classes were taught in English and German, making it the first bilingual college as well. And among the first students was Richea Gratz, the first Jewish female college student in the country. What a bunch of firsts! Unfortunately, the coed policy was dropped soon after the school opened, and the place didn't see another female student until 182 years had passed.

In 1836, Marshall College was founded in Mercersburg, Pennsylvania, and named after John Marshall, Chief Justice of the Supreme Court. It flourished, and its method of teaching became nationally famous as the Mercersburg theology.

As time went on, however, both schools suffered declining enrollment and were in danger of closing. In 1853 Marshall College moved to Lancaster and merged with Franklin College. The new school eventually became known as Franklin and Marshall College and grew into the 2,200-student college that it is today.

Even though the school weathered the Civil War, World War I, and World War II and has a rich and varied history going back to the formation of this country, it has accumulated only a select few of ghosts.

Diagnothian Hall, which was used as a hospital during the Civil War, is said to have "presences." At Wohlsen House, an impish spirit likes to turn off all the lights in the building at once. If you call out, "Knock it off, Bob!" the lights will come back on.

Over in South Franklin Dormitory in the late 1970s, a young woman found that the rigorous workload and pace of college life were just too much. Away from all of her friends and family, she took her life in her third-floor room. When winter finals approach, people hear screams in the night that aren't coming from students frustrated by all-night cram sessions. A spectral female figure wanders the hallways carrying a physics tome. Blood drips down the wall in the dorm room where the suicide took place.

Pennsylvania's Haunted Route 30

The Fulton Opera House

12 North Prince Street

Lancaster

When the Fulton Opera House is supposedly empty, workers hear unearthly screams. And no, these sounds are not coming from the throats of would-be opera singers. You see, it isn't so much that the building is haunted (though it is) as that the very ground it is built on is haunted.

Ed Kelemen

The Fulton Opera House has stood on this spot for over 150 years and has had its boards trod upon by the greatest of the great in the history of entertainment. Theatrical giants have appeared here. The royal family of the stage, the Barrymores, acted here, as did Sarah Bernhardt (known as the Divine Sarah), Al Jolson, W. C. Fields, Alfred Lunt, and Irene Dunne. A bushy-browed, white-haired gentleman with the stage name of Mark Twain offered up his pithy, homespun, view of Americana from this very stage. Edward and John Wilkes Booth were both famous tragedians who appeared here long before John's fame turned to infamy. The building's namesake, Robert Fulton, inventor of the steamship, watches over all from his statue in a niche three floors above Prince Street.

This Grand Old Lady, the oldest continuously operating theater in the country, is one of only eight named National Historic Landmarks.

Long before theatergoers were held in thrall, this spot was home to a more captive audience. The original Lancaster County Jail sat on this spot and held a full house of prisoners in chains and cells.

The early 1760s were a turbulent and dangerous time in Pennsylvania. The French and Indian War had just come to a close, and the victorious British were heavy-handed in enforcing their victory. Chief Pontiac of the Ottawa Tribe, a respected statesman, was able to form a loose-knit confederation of tribes of the Ohio, Illinois, and Great Lakes regions. Their intended purpose was to drive both the British soldiers and the British settlers out of the ancestral lands that had been stolen from them. This uprising came to be known as Pontiac's War and was noteworthy for its ruthlessness and treachery.

Scalping, an atrocity introduced by the British, became commonplace, as did the massacre of prisoners and bystanders and the targeting of civilians. The most infamous of these was when British officers at Fort Pitt provided Indians with blankets infected with smallpox in the hope that Indian families would be killed by the disease.

On top of everything else, the Governor of Pennsylvania, James Hamilton, refused to send troops to the rescue of the frontier people. This caused the formation of impromptu and informally led militia groups throughout the commonwealth. In no time, instead of protecting citizens, these groups became nothing more than murderers dedicated to the eradication of Native Americans from Pennsylvania.

One of the most vicious of these groups was known as the Paxton (or Paxtang) Boys. It was composed of over 200 men recruited by Reverend John Elder of Paxton Presbyterian Church near Harrisburg. This group quickly disintegrated from a protective unit to one devoted to the killing of all Indians. Peaceful or warlike, it made no difference to them. Maybe this is the origin of that racist saying, "The only good Indian is a dead Indian."

The Reverend Elder was fixated on eliminating a native who went by the name of Captain Bull. He was certainly a bane to peaceful existence and was responsible for the deaths of numerous settlers in Berks County. The Reverend set the rangers, as the Paxton Boys liked to call themselves, on the trail of Captain Bull. These self-styled rangers claimed that they had traced a number of Captain Bull's warriors to a place known as Conestoga. The Susquehannock Indians who lived in Conestoga were a peaceful community and they had been converted to Christianity by Moravian missionaries.

In the meantime, John Penn had replaced James Hamilton as Governor of Pennsylvania. The Reverend Elder immediately petitioned him, asking that all the Indians be removed from Pennsylvania. The Governor wrote back: "The faith of this government is pledged for their protection. I cannot remove them without adequate cause." This wasn't what the good reverend wanted to hear, so he sent the Paxton Boys out to do what the government wouldn't.

At dawn on a frigid December morning, the Indians in the little Conestoga village awakened to the sound of fifty armed men heading their way. Knowing what was likely to come, they ran out of their homes wearing only the clothes on their backs, carrying the younger children. Old people stumbled and fell in the snow.

The so-called rangers held Indians in such contempt that they felt that it would be wasteful to spend bullets and powder on them. They rode the fleeing people down and clubbed them to death. One small boy was swept up by a ranger and had his head bashed against a tree.

Fourteen of the villagers escaped and sought protection from their Moravian benefactors. Some of the survivors continued on to Philadelphia. Those old people and children who couldn't travel fast sought protection from the sheriff in Lancaster. The sheriff housed them in the jail, locking the cells for their protection. Surely this old fortress could prevent break-ins as well as breakouts.

Captain Lazarus Stewart of the Paxton Boys somehow learned that Captain Bull was among the survivors in the Lancaster jail. He convinced his men to ride on to Lancaster so that they could demand that Captain Bull be released into their custody, ostensibly to go to Carlisle for trial.

They found no one of authority at the jail. However, the jailer, before his rapid departure, had left the keys lying in plain sight on his desk.

The Paxton Boys entered the cells where the Indians had taken refuge and slaughtered them. The old people threw their bodies over the children to protect them, but to no avail. Their attempts to defend the children only fed the vigilantes' blood lust. Every man, woman, and child in those cells was beaten, stomped, slashed, and hacked to death. There were no survivors. The infamous Captain Bull, who was the start of much of the antagonism in the area, died in the slaughter.

The final few survivors made it to Philadelphia and sought sanctuary. When the Paxton Boys trailed them, a contingent of armed citizens led by Benjamin Franklin refused them entry. Those last survivors lived out their years in Philadelphia. When they died, so did the Susquehannock Indian tribe. The Reverend Elder got his wish.

That jail was razed and the Fulton Opera House was built on the blood-soaked grounds. The only remains from that terrible day, December 27, 1763, are the old gates of the prison in the basement and a simple plaque on the wall listing the names of the victims.

The unearthly screams that workers hear may be coming from the mouths of children and old folk in their dying throes. Few people can spend any extended time in the basement of the opera house. They feel the presence of the murdered Indians and an unnerving sense of silent watching, watching, watching . . . .

Ed Kelemen

Upstairs, in the Opera House proper, the haunts aren't as reticent. Up in the fly of the theater, where all the rigging is done, is the last wooden grid of any theater in the country. Stagehands raising and lowering scenery have seen the ghost of a woman up in that gridwork, but no one knows who she is or why she is there.

On one side of the stage is another ethereal being, a woman who walks up and down the stairwell there. One late night a director on stage mentioned that he would like to see a ghost, just once. His colleagues just nodded and went back to work. A few minutes later, one coworker called softly to him, "Carl, turn around."

When Carl turned around, he saw nothing. He was told, "You missed her. She just went down those steps."

Another time, the cast of a play in rehearsal were standing offstage when they saw a hazy outline moving down the house where the center aisle had once been. The center aisle had been eliminated when the theater was restored.

One time, the lighting gaffer on the second balcony noticed an elderly black man take a seat in that balcony, which was closed to the public for that performance. No matter, she thought. He must be related to a cast member. It was common for family members to watch performances from way up there. When the play was over, she turned to ask him how he had enjoyed the performance. He was gone. Where he had gone was a mystery since he would have had to pass by her to leave. Later she told the only black actor in the production about it. He smiled and said, "Oh, that's my father. He's been dead for ten years."

Pennsylvania's Haunted Route 30

History, haunts, lavish productions, stars of stage and screen--this old dowager has it all. If you would like to visit, give them a call at (717) 397-7425.

***

Back on Old Route 30, now called Lancaster Pike, let's keep on our eastward journey.

Ed Kelemen

Main Street

Strasburg

Let's take a turn south on PA Route 896 and visit Strasburg. This little town of one square mile has more original eighteenth-century buildings than Williamsburg, Virginia. If you are a railroad buff, you probably already know about the short-line railroad that was built by the residents nearly two centuries ago and is still in operation today.

When you are sitting at the traffic signal on Main Street and hear the rhythmic clip-clop of horses' hooves on the pavement, take a minute to look around. It's true that in Lancaster County you'll see many Amish families going to and fro in their black horse-drawn buggies, but that may not be what you're hearing. . .

From time to time, a carriage full of soldiers in full Civil War uniforms rides right down the middle of Main Street on their way home for a furlough before going back to the dangers of war. They are not re-enactors. If you watch long enough, they will fade into nothingness and the creaks and clip-clops will disappear.

Stop at the John Funk House on West Main Street to check out the antiques and other things for sale. You just may be waited on by John Funk himself. He has been known to do that when the regular help is occupied with other customers. You may even hear whispered conversations between John and his wife. The only thing out of the ordinary is that neither John nor his wife has been alive in the customary sense for many, many years.

You may want to stop at the National Toy Train Museum, the Choo-choo Barn, or the Amish Village, or take a ride on the nation's oldest short-line railroad. Whatever you do, don't leave without sampling some of the scrumptious food available at the historic restaurants in town.

A candlelight walking tour of the haunted places in Strasburg is available during most of the year. Check out www.ghosttour.net/strasburg.html for details, or give them a call at (717) 667-6687.

***

When you've seen the sights of Strasburg, head back north the couple of miles to Route 30 and continue eastward along that haunted highway.

Ed Kelemen

The Ship Inn

Intersection of Business Route 30 and Ship Lane, Exton

Built in 1796, the Ship Inn has hosted hungry, thirsty travelers for over 200 years. Although the place has been completely renovated inside and out, it retains its original configuration. The food and drink must be excellent; at least one customer from the 1800s can't tear himself away. Both restaurant staff and customers have seen a man standing in the hallway who vanishes as soon as he is noticed. Perhaps it is the same fellow who takes a seat at a table but disappears when he is approached.

The second floor is definitely haunted by a less than friendly spirit. Staff members experience a feeling of being closely watched, as though someone is standing directly behind them, when they are up there alone.

Although no one has ever been harmed, several members of the staff refuse to go up there due to the intensity of the feeling.

If you don't mind being joined by someone who should have left a couple of centuries ago, sit down, order some great steak or seafood and look around for the guy wearing early 1800s garb, but look quickly, and remember, he's bashful.

Ed Kelemen

The Radnor Hotel

591 East Lancaster Avenue

St. Davids

The Pennsylvania Railroad's main line originally ran northwest from downtown Philadelphia, paralleling US Route 30 (also called Lancaster Avenue and originally called the Philadelphia and Lancaster Turnpike). In 1913, when the Lincoln Highway was designated the first transcontinental highway, it was incorporated into Lancaster Avenue.

Since the Pennsylvania Railroad's main line gave the wealthiest citizens ready, reliable, and rapid access to the north and west suburbs, those affluent suburbs became known as the Main Line.

The Radnor Hotel is an example of the upscale, full-service hotels found on the Main Line. Its accommodations and amenities may be why at least one former occupant has decided to stay. She likes Room 309. Corporeal guests who have stayed in that room have awakened at night to find her diaphanous spirit hovering over the bed. The ghost then slides (some accounts say crawls) down the wall and disappears through the wall into the hallway. Hotel employees and guests of the hotel have heard strange noises coming from Room 309 when it is supposed to be vacant.

So if you want a good night's sleep, ask for any room but 309. If, on the other hand, you would like to see or even speak to a denizen from the beyond, then by all means request that room.

***

A little farther east on Route 30, we come to King of Prussia Road. Let's take a left onto it and travel along for two miles to Cabrini College.

Ed Kelemen

Cabrini College

610 King of Prussia Road

Radnor

Cabrini College was founded in 1957 by the Missionary Sisters of the Sacred Heart of Jesus and named for Saint Frances Xavier Cabrini, the founder of the order. The first year saw 43 female students cross the threshold into the realm of higher education. Thirteen years later, male students were invited to apply. The college has been coeducational ever since.

The site of the college was originally called Woodcrest, the estate of Dr. John Dorrance, who invented the process for condensed soup and became the president of Campbell's Soup Company. The sisters purchased the property in 1953, originally named it Villa Cabrini, and used it as an orphanage. They didn't bargain on the ghosts that came with the purchase.

John Dorrance was a widower who lived at Woodcrest with the apple of his eye, his daughter Lucy. Nothing was too good for her, and nothing was out of the reach of Dr. Dorrance's purse. One of the things the good doctor indulged in was a fine stable of horses.

One of the stable boys was Xavier, a handsome fellow who paid extra attention to Lucy's rides, lest she get injured by too spirited a mount. You know what can happen when two young people are thrown together. The pair fell in love, much to the consternation of Dr. Dorrance, who did not want an unrefined son-in-law smelling of horseflesh and worse. He forbade his daughter to see the stable boy.

Xavier was so heartbroken that he hanged himself among the horses in the stable, which is now Grace Hall. John Dorrance's daughter was now at the end of her rope. She had just lost the love of her life, and she was expecting a child. She saw no way out of the disgrace but to throw herself off the balcony of the mansion.

Lucy wears a blue or white dress and has long flowing blonde hair that is swirled by the breeze. Late evening on the day of the first snowfall finds her wandering the area in front of Woodcrest Hall, supposedly looking for the child who perished when she plunged from the balcony.

I sincerely hope that you are not so unfortunate as to meet Mr. Dorrance himself. He skulks about the campus of Cabrini College, mainly on the roads and driveways, wearing a top hat and a long, flowing black cape. He appears out of nowhere right in front of your car. Before you have time to react, you will run him down. You and your passengers will feel the sickening thump of his body hitting the front of the car, then those stomach-wrenching bumps and crunches as first the front, then the rear, tires run over his body. Of course you'll stop immediately to give aid to the poor victim, but when you investigate, you will find no evidence of an accident other than footprints in the snow leading up to the point of impact. Will you feel relieved or frightened by your trip into the paranormal? Will you forever drive more slowly on long, winding driveways?

There is a tale of a secret tunnel leading from the mansion to Grace Hall. This tunnel was supposedly constructed so the butler could travel between the two buildings without having to go outside on bitterly cold days. I think it more likely that a butler who complained of the cold would be told to put on a coat. Nevertheless, the legend of the tunnel has persisted, even though all attempts to find it have failed. The tale goes that, if you find it and travel its length, you will come to a portrait leaning up against the wall at the far end. If you look upon that portrait, you will lose your mind and your memory for several days.

Even though the tunnel has not been found, people who have investigated the basement of the mansion have encountered cold spots.

Female students living in Woodcrest Hall have experienced what they call the Old Hag syndrome. When they are quietly studying alone in their room, they hear voices whispering around them, just below their threshold of understanding. Electronic items turn themselves on and off at will, sometimes even when unplugged. And while the students are in bed, a heavy weight descends upon them, preventing them from moving or speaking.

***

Let's get back on Lancaster Avenue and head toward the city, stopping at our next institution of higher learning.

Ed Kelemen

V

In the City of Brotherly Love

Villanova University

600 East Lancaster Avenue

Villanova

Villanova University had a rocky beginning. It was founded in 1841 by two Augustinian friars from St. Augustine's Church in Philadelphia, 12 miles to the east.

In 1844, during a series of anti-Catholic riots called the Philadelphia nativist riots, St. Augustine's Church was burned. This created financial difficulties that led to the temporary closing of the school. A decade later, the school was once again closed because a shortage of Catholic clergy in Philadelphia caused severe staffing problems. It remained closed for the duration of the Civil War, though it has been open ever since September 1865.

The iconic view of Villanova University is the twin spires of St. Thomas of Villanova church, which fronts Lancaster Avenue, our old Route 30.

Behind those spires lies Alumni Hall, where the floors and walls creak when there is nothing around to place extra weight on them. Students have awakened during the night with the same problem that students up the road at Cabrini College have felt: some unknown force is pressing them down on the bed. No matter how they try, their struggles are futile. They cannot move. After a few minutes the force abruptly ceases and they are no longer restrained.

This building was used as a hospital during the Civil War. Maybe it is reliving those horrible moments when a soldier had to be restrained as an amputation was performed without anesthetic.

In the middle of the night, people are summoned by an unseen woman. Trying to find her is as futile as trying to catch whoever is making the nocturnal footfalls in the hallways.

Nearby St. Mary's Hall was once a convent. Student lore says that a nun hanged herself there. Students and maintenance staff often hear a radio playing loudly in the evening. When they go to complain, not only is the room unoccupied, but the offending radio is unplugged.

Laughter and splashing are heard coming from the pool. When someone goes to investigate, the water is untouched and the pool area is empty.

Vigorous activity is heard in the kitchen, as though a banquet is being prepared--but the kitchen is empty. And a phantom in the music room entertains listeners by playing the piano.

Lest anyone attribute these hauntings to collegiate pranksters, many of them happen between terms, when no students are present.

Bryn Mawr College

101 North Merion Avenue

Bryn Mawr

Just two blocks north of Route 30 in Bryn Mawr is a stately old college named after the little suburb where it is located. It was founded in 1885 by Dr. Joseph W. Taylor as an institution of higher learning for "the advanced education of females." Although part of his vision was that the school would instruct its students in the ways of the Religious Society of Friends (Quakers), it became a secular school in 1893.

In 1907, Lillian Vickers was a 19-year-old, impressionable girl, possibly away from home for the first time in her life. She was a resident of Merion Hall (called College Hall in those days). Somehow she became convinced that she had contracted leprosy. She may have had an intense case of adolescent acne; nobody knows. No matter how many doctors examined her and found nothing medically wrong, she was unswerving in her conviction.

She researched the disease as much as she was able in those pre-Internet days and decided to eradicate it by applying either alcohol or kerosene to her entire body. She attempted to affect this cure on December 21, 1907. She got too close to an ignition source and burst into flames. With a bloodcurdling scream, she rushed from the bathroom and ran down the hall afire. Other students smothered the flames with blankets, but she died from her burns a few hours later.

The intensity of this tragic accident seems to have bound her to the building. Residents hear screams and pleas in the hallway, and see wavering lights, but no physical presence is ever found.

No one knows whether Bryn Mawr's most famous graduate, Katherine Hepburn, ever heard the haunt. Possibly Kate was too busy starting the tradition of skinny-dipping in the Cloisters to stay awake after long hours of study.

Rosemont College

1400 Montgomery Avenue

Bryn Mawr

Just a few blocks away from Bryn Mawr College is Rosemont College, yet another school formed by a religious order for the purpose of educating young Christian women. This one was opened by the Catholic Society of the Holy Child Jesus in 1921. In 2009, the college started accepting male students for undergraduate courses.

Rosemont College is a peaceful place and hasn't been afflicted with the turmoil and tragedy that was foisted on older institutions of learning. It didn't suffer through the religious riots of the 1840s, the Civil War, financial panics of the 1800s, or World War I. It is also lucky enough not to have had students who were emotionally distressed to the point of suicide or who died in tragic accidents.

Thus, it cannot lay claim to screaming haunts running through the hall afire or ghosts who have taken a lover's leap from a high balcony. There are no glum specters roaming the byways of the school, popping out to scare motorists witless.

However, students have seen nebulous, misty beings in the shadowy hallways at night and heard slamming doors when there is no one around to slam them.

Ed Kelemen

***

Another two miles along Route 30 (Lancaster Avenue), brings us to Montgomery Avenue. Go left, and in two miles we will come to what was once the most haunted place in Philadelphia, if not the entire state, the General Wayne Inn.

General Wayne Inn

Now the Chabad of the Main Line

625 Montgomery Avenue

Merion

I say "once" when referring to the General Wayne Inn because the inn has since been purchased by a synagogue, and I sincerely doubt if the Chabad Center for Jewish Life at the General Wayne Inn will welcome curiosity seekers in a place of worship and peace. The stated aim of the Chabad of the Main Line is to welcome everyone "regardless of background or affiliation to participate in Jewish programming and community events that will provide meaning, engender communication and bring sanctity to Jewish life in the Main Line." It says nothing about ghost hunting, so please respect this now hallowed ground. Let us keep our observations outside and from a distance.

The General Wayne Inn was named after General "Mad Anthony" Wayne, who died in Erie, Pennsylvania, in 1796 and was buried near the Presque Isle blockhouse. There he lay for a dozen years until his daughter prevailed upon her brother Isaac to retrieve his remains and have them reburied in the family cemetery in Radnor. Well, when they dug him up, they discovered that he hadn't decomposed as much as expected. There just wasn't enough room for him in the light sulky Issac had traveled in. So the flesh was boiled off the bones, the bones were put in a box strapped to the back of the sulky, and General Wayne's bones were transported back to the eastern end of the state along a bumpy, rocky track that followed what is now US Route 322. Along the road, a number of the bones bounced out of the box and were lost. Every year on New Year's Day, Mad Anthony Wayne gallops along that road, in full Revolutionary War regalia, looking for those bones to make his skeleton whole.

The inn opened in 1704 and has entertained such historic figures as George Washington, the Marquis de Lafayette, Redcoats, Continentals, and even Hessians. In 1795, General Anthony stopped at the Inn and held a three-day celebration of his latest military victory. Right then and there, the inn was renamed the General Wayne Inn. Edgar Allan Poe was a habitué, enjoying the Inn's signature dishes, squirrel ragout and pigeon stew. Part of his famous poem "The Raven" reportedly was penned there.

This place opened for business over 300 years ago. Three centuries is enough time to accumulate some hauntings, and the intense history of the area didn't hurt, either.

All the turbulent history of the place has resulted in nearly 20 individual ghosts on the premises. It is a good thing the building is rather large, or they would be really crowded.

A Hessian soldier, Wilhelm, killed during a Revolutionary War battle stayed in the cellar, mortified that he had been buried in his undergarments. Wilhelm said that he couldn't rest until he was buried properly in his beautiful uniform. Another Hessian soldier, Ludwig by name, made his presence known in 1976 and begged that his bones, which were buried in the cellar, be properly reinterred. A search of the cellar found a hidden room that did indeed contain the bones. Ludwig was reburied and hasn't been seen since.

A group of Hessian soldiers wander in and out of the place, along with an African American and an Indian. Various spirits sit at the bar and walk about the inn like regular patrons and employees of the establishment. The Hessians have a history of mischievous acts.

A little boy ghost who had lost his mother wouldn't stop crying long enough for investigators to determine how to help him.

Two young women from the early 1800s, Sadie and Sara, were entrusted with some valuable merchandise that was never called for, and they fear that they may be accused of stealing the item. What these valuable items were, nobody seems to know--or maybe they have guilty consciences.

During a séance held at the inn during 1972, one of the haunts commented that the tea was beyond comparison, but the spirituous drinks weren't quite up to his standards. Another said the beer was below expectations as well. They weren't even paying!

In 1996, the co-owners, Guy Sileo and James Webb, were experiencing financial difficulties running the inn. This caused so much conflict between them that on December 27, 1996, Webb was found shot to death in his office. Sileo was arrested, but assistant chef Felicia Moyse, who was having an affair with Sileo, provided an alibi. She said he was with her at the time of the murder. She committed suicide in February 1997, and Sileo immediately changed his story, claiming that she had committed the crime. Guy Sileo was convicted of murder and sentenced to life in prison. His latest attempt at a retrial was overturned in 2011.

That brings us full circle. The General Wayne Inn is no more. Perhaps now that it has become a place of worship, its restless spirits have found solace and contentment. If so, they may now accept the fact that they are no longer of this world.

***

Let's leave them to whatever peace they have found and head on into the City of Philadelphia.

Eastern State Penitentiary

2027 Fairmont Avenue

Philadelphia

We digress here. Eastern State Penitentiary is not on Route 30, but no attempt to visit ethereal beings in this great city would be complete without a visit to this ex-hotel for offenders. It was hailed as the greatest humanitarian reform in handling prisoners when it opened in 1829, its system of solitary confinement and strict discipline drove hundreds of inmates mad. Many never left, even after it was closed in 1970.

There isn't enough space to mention all the haunts of

the penitentiary. Just remember, no ghost hunting visit to eastern Pennsylvania is complete without a visit here.

Check out its website for details and hours. You won't be disappointed. If you visit this warehouse of lost souls, wear comfy shoes, watch for uneven pavement, and take something to keep hydrated.

Additional information is available at www.easternstate.org.

***

Three hundred-plus miles finally bring us to historic Philadelphia, where our forebears trod the sidewalks and famous personages satisfied their thirsts in the taverns. Here is where our great country was born--and where some citizens of that time remain.

Historic Philadelphia

Bonaparte's Court

260 South Ninth Street

Philadelphia

At this location in historic Philadelphia are four townhouses dating from the early 1800s. One of these was the home of Chloris Ingleby, who was famous for the provocative dances she performed in local waterfront taverns during the War of 1812.

Another of the houses in this little area known as Bonaparte's Court is called the Bonaparte House. It got that name from the time that Joseph Bonaparte spent in residence there. You may have heard of Joseph's younger brother, Napoleon.

Amedee La Fourcade was the steward of the house of Joseph Bonaparte. It was inevitable that he meet Chloris since they lived in such close proximity. It wasn't inevitable that she fall in love with him, but she did. And he returned her affections, giving her the impression that she might count on the future surname of La Fourcade. After a year had passed, he returned to the isle of Corsica to marry a "respectable" woman. Chloris lost it. She stowed away on the ship, but she was discovered before it sailed and was imprisoned in the barn at the rear of Bonaparte House. She escaped, breaking free of her captors and running down the alley as fast as she could to catch the ship before it sailed. The Bonaparte staff claimed that she escaped, but in fact they shot her in the back and she died in that alley. Local lore has it that her body is walled up in the barn.

She wanders about the area, a young lady in period dress. She could be a skilled re-enactor but for the anguished look on her face as she searches for her lying lover. Does she still love him, or is she determined to mete out his just deserts?

St Peter's Episcopal Church Cemetery

Fourth and Pine Streets

Philadelphia

St. Peter's Church was built in 1758 on land donated to the church by the sons of William Penn, for whom Pennsylvania is named. George and Martha Washington frequently attended services, using Philadelphia Mayor Samuel Powel's box.

Its cemetery has graves of soldiers who served in the Revolutionary War, the War of 1812, the Civil War, WWI, and WWII. You can tell which war a veteran fought in by the number of stars on the flag adorning his or her resting place.

Other notables to be found beneath the ground here include Colonel John Nixon, who gave the first public reading of the Declaration of Independence on July 8, 1776, and Revolutionary War hero Commodore John Hazelwood. They were joined by painter Charles Wilson Peale, who painted the first portrait of George Washington, and Vice President George Mifflin Dallas, who gave his name to the city of Dallas, Texas. Stephen Decatur, the hero of the Battle of Tripoli, has also found his eternal rest here. There are also the graves of eight Indian chiefs who were stricken down with smallpox when visiting the city in 1793 for a meeting with George Washington.

The Indian chiefs, perhaps because they were interred in a nontribal burial ground, are a bit restless and sometimes wander the area after dark.

You may hear late at night the clip-clop of horses' hooves on the cobbled pathway, along with the creaks and groans of an unseen carriage pulling up to the door of the church for a nocturnal funeral.

An African-American gentleman in full colonial uniform patrols the cemetery at night, maybe to prevent looters or other trespassers from defiling the graves. So remember, if you decide to walk these hallowed grounds, be it day or night, behave with the decorum that this place deserves.

***

A stroll along Sixth Street will take us to Washington Square, long the domain of the dead.

Washington Square
Walnut Street between Sixth and Seventh
Philadelphia

Washington Square is one of the original five squares that were laid out in 1682 when William Penn was planning the city of Philadelphia. At that time, it was called Southeast Square, since the Quakers did not believe in naming places for people.

Its beginnings quickly became ignominious when, in 1704 it was designated a, "Potter's Field." Strangers, the destitute, and prisoners were buried here for the next 90 years. Generally, those unfortunate to be interred here were simply wrapped in canvas and buried with neither coffin, ceremony, nor marker.

The Joshua Carpenter family purchased a private family burial ground, smack dab in the center of the square. That was because a female family member had committed suicide and their church refused to allow her to be buried in the sanctified church cemetery. Suicide was an unacceptable way to die.

Rites similar to the Mexican, "Day of The Dead," were practiced in the burial ground by members of the black community. They went to the graves of friends and relatives, leaving offerings of food and rum. Was this possibly a transported ceremony from Africa or the Caribbean? Slaves were also allowed to use the square during holidays, holding dances and honoring the, "sleeping dust," below.

Come the mid-1700s, the square was found to be

good pastureland and was leased for that purpose by Jasper Carpenter. Persons other than myself have mentioned that it was well fertilized. In any case, the pastoral period was short-lived. Starting in 1776, the bodies of members of the Colonial Army were buried here. There were so many that they were buried in caskets piled one on top of another. This was done along the 7th Street side of the square until the huge pit dug there was filled with the coffins. Then another pit was dug along the southern side of the square and filled in the same way.

In 1777 the British captured Philadelphia and used the Walnut Street Jail on the square to house prisoners. What with overcrowding, malnutrition, and less than ideal treatment many more poor souls found their way beneath the earth in the square. Once again, during a Yellow Fever epidemic in 1793, the square was used as a mass grave for the numerous citizens of the city who perished from that ailment.

It was allowed to lie fallow until 1815 when improvements were begun that transformed it into a public park. Ten years later, in 1825, it was named Washington Square in honor of our nation's first president.

No matter the attempts to lighten up the area and convert it into a beautiful pastoral setting for city dwellers, its original use, or misuse, comes through. A Quaker woman named Leah patrols the park to protect it from grave robbers, even though she hasn't actually had a material existence in over 200 years. She has been seen by many ghost tour guests and even a Philadelphia Police Officer. A paranormal investigator suffered a heart attack after experiencing something in the park. Speculation aside, it isn't known whether the heart attack was connected to his experience, or a coincidence.

And here's something to carry away with you. Notice how all the nearby streets and many of the city's other parks are populated with the homeless sleeping on benches, under trees and so forth. Then take a look around Washington Square- they avoid this place.

***

Now, after this long cross-state trek we come to the last of our haunted locations. We will walk four blocks along walnut street toward the river. Then, a left on 2nd Street and a few more yards will find us at a place where people, from our founding fathers up to and including ourselves, have quenched their thirst.

Ed Kelemen

CITY TAVERN
138 South Second Street

Philadelphia

Built in 1772, the City Tavern has experienced a rich and varied history. During our country's formative years it was the unofficial meeting place for the Continental Congress. Early habitués included George Washington, Thomas Jefferson, Benjamin Franklin, and John Adams. It was to the City Tavern that Paul Revere rode to announce that the British had closed the port of Boston. I'm not surprised that the first place he would stop after a

300-plus mile ride on horseback was a tavern to quaff a pint of ale and drive the dust from his throat. Come to think of it, we have just trekked 300-plus miles to get here. So what do you say we stop in for one of the tavern's excellent historic brews?

On your way in, take a good look at the facade, the building, and its surroundings. For most of its existence it hasn't looked this pristine. In 1834, a wedding reception was held here. Food was plentiful and libations flowed freely, but at some point the celebration turned into tragedy when a fire ignited and quickly grew out of control. A number of the celebrants burned to death in the conflagration, including the bride.

After that, the owners tried to make a go of it, but a pall hung over the building and it had been severely damaged by the fire. Finally it was demolished due to unprofitability and structural instability.

For the nation's bicentennial in 1976, the City Tavern rose from the ashes of its past much like the fabled Phoenix. An exact replica opened on the very spot where the original tavern stood. Since then, it has received accolade after accolade, consistently being named one of Philadelphia's top ten restaurants.

The tavern's original employees must approve of the replica. Its oldest haunt is a waiter who was killed there in a barroom brawl. He was an innocent bystander and rumor has it that he is still upset that nobody was ever brought to justice for his death. He makes regular appearances in the barroom in his bloody white shirt. Dishes move and silverware jangles all on their own--or possibly with his spectral assistance.

And what of that young woman who perished in the fire at her wedding reception? She must also approve of the new digs. She has come back, perhaps to relive the happiest--and the last--day of her life. Still in her wedding gown, she roams the hallways and hangs out in the barroom.

If you decide to stop in for a luncheon experience washed down with a tasty heirloom brew, ask your waitstaff to seat you in the haunted area. You just may meet one of these denizens of the dead. Don't worry, they won't try to mooch a beer or a sandwich from you.

finis

Visiting the ghosts along Route 30

As you read this book and travel the route, you just may want to stop at some of these haunted places and say hello to the ghosts located there. They'll give you a cold shoulder or even a warm welcome. Dining with an otherworldly dweller or raising a toast to his or her afterlife could be an enjoyable way to spend some time.

Touring a haunted museum, cemetery, or battlefield is a wonderful experience. How about attempting to sleep the night at a haunted hotel? Want to see if specters share the stage with the actors at a couple of famous theaters?

Most places along the highway are open to the public and can be visited nearly at will. I have tried to avoid listing places where the occupants don't welcome visitors. The locations of those places who don't I have deliberately made a bit vague.

Some places have specific hours, others are actual places of business, and some charge admission.

To ease the burden of making arrangements to rub elbows with the dead, but lively people in these places, here is a list of them, along with their websites and contact information.

Now, as we all know, time changes everything. All this information was viable at press time. But just in case, verify it before showing up unannounced at any of these locations.

Point State Park
www.dcnr.state.pa.us/stateparks/findapark/point/
Fort Pitt Museum
heinzhistorycenter.org/secondary.aspx?id=296
(412)281-9284
Fort Pitt Blockhouse
(412)471-1764

William Penn Hotel
www.omnihotels.com/FindAHotel/PittsburghWilliamPenn.aspx
(412)281-7100
530 William Penn Place
Pittsburgh, PA 15219

The Pittsburgh Playhouse
www.pittsburghplayhouse.com
(412)392-8000
222 Craft Avenue
Pittsburgh, PA 15213

University of Pittsburgh Nationality Rooms
www.nationalityrooms.pitt.edu
(412)624-6001
4200 Fifth Ave
Pittsburgh, PA 15260

Carnegie Library&Museum of Natural History
www.carnegiemnh.org/visit/hours/
4400 Forbes Ave.
Pittsburgh, PA 15213

Frick Art and Historical Center
www.thefrickpittsburgh.org
(412)371-0600
7227 Reynolds Ave
Pittsburgh, PA 152085

Lincoln Highway Heritage Corridor
www.lhhc.org
(724)879-4241
Lincoln Highway Experience
3435 State Route 30 East
Latrobe, PA 15650

Ligonier Tavern
www.ligoniertavern.com
(724)238-4831
139 West Main Street
Ligonier, PA 15658

Fort Ligonier
www.fortligonier.org
(724)238-9701
200 South Market St.
Ligonier, PA 15658

Flight 93 National Memorial
www.nps.gov/flni/index.htm
(814)893-6322
6424 Lincoln Highway
Stoystown, PA 15563

Jean Bonnet Tavern
www.jeanbonnettavern.com
(814)623-2250
6048 Lincoln Highway
Bedford, PA 15522

Old Bedford Village
www.oldbedfordvillage.com
(814)623-1156
220 Sawblade Rd.
Bedford, PA 15522

The Cashtown Inn
www.cashtowninn.com
(717)334-9722
1325 Old Route 30
Cashtown, PA 17310

Herr Tavern and Publick House
www.herrtavern.com
 (717)334-4332
900 Chambersburg Rd.
Gettysburg, PA 17325

Getttysburg National Military Park
www.nps.gov/gett/index.htm
(717)334-1124, extension 8023
Gettysburg, PA

The Accomac Inn
www.accomacinn.com
(717)252-1521
6330 River Drive
York, PA 17406

The Fulton Opera House
www.thefulton.org
(717)397-7425
12 N. Prince St.
Lancaster, PA 17603

The Ship Inn
www.shipinn.net
(610)363-7200
693 East Lincoln Highway
Exton, PA 19341

Eastern State Penitentiary
www.easternstate.org
(215)236-3300
2027 Fairmont Ave.
Philadelphia, PA 19130

City Tavern
www.citytavern.com
(215)413-1443
138 South 2nd Street
Philadelphia, PA 19106

ABOUT THE AUTHOR

Ed Kelemen is a writer, columnist, and playwright who lives in a small West Central Pennsylvania town with his wife, two of five sons, a pair of humongous dogs and a clutch of attitude-ridden cats. His article and short stories have appeared in numerous local, regional, and national publications. Visit with him at www.ekelemen.com.